THE

WASHINGTON

Despotism Dissected

IN ARTICLES FROM THE

METROPOLITAN RECORD.

FIFTH EDITION

New York:
OFFICE OF THE METROPOLITAN RECORD,
No. 419 Broadway.
1864.

THE WASHINGTON DESPOTISM

DISSECTED

IN

ARTICLES

FROM

The Metropolitan Record.

NEW YORK:
OFFICE OF THE METROPOLITAN RECORD,
No. 419 Broadway.

1863.

TO THE PUBLIC.

In consequence of the great demand for the numbers of the Record containing the articles enumerated in the index, the supply was soon exhausted. As the papers are still called for, the publication of this pamphlet is intended to obviate the difficulty.

It can be had of all newsdealers throughout the country

CONTENTS.

PAGE

The United States Converted into a Military Despotism.......... 7
Can a Disunion Administration Restore the Union?............. 17
A Great Statesman Speaking to the People..................... 26
Grounds of Impeachment of the President...................... 29
The Effects of Abolitionism.................................. 33
What is a Loyal Leaguer?..................................... 36
Grand Patriotic Demonstration................................ 39
Some Plain Talk.. 54
"Nobody's Hurt."... 58
Peace!... 61
Model Resolutions for the Loyal Leaguers..................... 68
What the War is carried on for............................... 71
A New Joke—Is it the President's?............................ 72
The Abolition Policy of the Administration, and what it has Accomplished.......... 74
The Statesman of the Revolution on the Right of Coercion....... 80
The Sovereignty of the States................................ 87
The Northern Plague.. 92
The Letter of Governor Seymour............................... 95
A Poland in the United States................................ 100
The Future... 102
Which is the most Humiliating—Peace or War?.................. 113
The Conscription... 118
The Administration Telegraph; or. How it is Done............. 121

ARTICLES

FROM THE

METROPOLITAN RECORD.

THE UNITED STATES CONVERTED INTO A MILITARY DESPOTISM.

THE CONSCRIPTION ACT THE LAST DEADLY BLOW AIMED AT POPULAR LIBERTY.

(*From the* METROPOLITAN RECORD, *March* 14, 1863.)

THE Congress which has so fatally misrepresented the Republic during the last two years has at length adjourned. It expired on the 4th instant, leaving behind it a memory that time can never efface, and fastening indelibly upon the history of the nation the blackest record the world has ever seen. It found the United States a free country, and it has left it a land of slaves. It was elected to do the behests of the people, and it has converted our servants into our masters, and our President into an autocrat, with power as great over the liberties of the people as that which the Czar of all the Russias possesses over his subjects. All this it has done, and more. It has rendered a union of fraternity an impossibility; it has again and again passed enactments violating the supreme law of the land; it has persistently refused to permit any inquiry to be made into the arbitrary arrests of loyal citizens; it has broken down State limits, and admitted bogus members as representatives who pretend to have been constitutionally elected, and in its last measure, the Conscription Act, it has put the liberties of the people in the hands of a man whose presidential career has proved that he never wanted the will to become the arbitrary master of this so-called Republic. With a persistence that the dread crisis through which the nation is passing could not affect nor alter, it has devoted all its energies to the destruction of an institution guaranteed by the Constitution itself; it has made the liberty of the white man only of secondary importance to that of the negro; it has lent its aid to the suppression of the liberty of the press by silently sanctioning the action of its subordinates in suspending the publication of several of the newspapers throughout the country. It has quietly looked on while our citizens have been dragged from their homes at the dead hour of night and flung into government bastiles; it has preferred the permanent disruption of the Union to its perpetuity with the institution of slavery preserved; it has knowingly and willfully set at naught the desires and intentions of the great conservative majority of the North, and in the passage of the Conscription Act it has been guilty of a most criminal violation of the sovereignty of the people as involved in the rights of the States.

This is the record left to us by a Congress which has done more to render the restoration of the Union impossible than all the acts of the most bitter and determined secessionists.

When the country could have been saved by the adoption in the Border State Convention of the Crittenden compromise—a compromise intended to secure to the South nothing but what it was justly entitled to—the leading members of both the Senate and House of Representatives employed all the force of their official character and position to secure the defeat of the measure. In its almost every act it proved to the South that it would be satisfied with nothing less than its unconditional submission and the extinction of slavery. It falsified its pledges made at the commencement of the war, that the immense military and naval resources of the country should be employed only in the restoration of the Union, and the re-establishment of the Constitution as the supreme law of the land.

But, as we have intimated, the crowning act of despotism, the most atrocious piece of legislation which it has perpetrated, is the Conscription Law, which is hardly less intolerable than that which has driven Poland into wide-spread insurrection. In this measure the radical and fanatical policy of Congress has reached its climax. That body, in its last days, attained the "bad eminence" to which it was so long aspiring; and its last act is the most deadly blow that has yet been aimed at the liberties of the people; it is the most envenomed shaft that has yet been hurled at the heart of the Republic, and if the people are untrue to themselves in this dire emergency, the freedom of the nation will be buried in the same grave in which Congress has interred all that remained of the Union.

One of the most remarkable features of this last effort to convert the Republic into a military despotism, is the entire abnegation of State sovereignty in the process by which the conscription is to be carried into operation. State limits and State sovereignty are ridden over rough-shod, and our Governors, the freely chosen magistrates of a free people, are to be treated as mere ciphers by the General Government.

In a word, all the citizens of New York liable to military duty under this law can be called upon by the President whenever he shall deem it necessary, and on the refusal of any one of these to obey the call, he "shall be deemed a deserter, be arrested by the Provost Marshal, and sent to the nearest military post for court-martial." If this is not the establishment of a military despotism, then we should like to know the true meaning of the words. We have no hesitation whatever in saying that this law is unconstitutional, and, of course, not binding upon any citizen of the United States; and since the mis-called National Legislature has so far exceeded its powers, the people must, under such circumstances, look for protection to the only authorities that can grant it, the Governors of their respective States. We owe allegiance as citizens of the State of New York to the constitution of that State, and in the exercise of his lawful authority we are solemnly bound by that obligation to sustain and support its Chief Magistrate, whom that constitution declares is the Commander-in-Chief of the military and naval forces of the State. If allegiance belongs to that regularly-constituted power which, in the general community, affords protection to life and property, then we say our loyalty is pre-eminently due to the State government. As to the Constitution of the United States, that instrument no longer affords protection to its citizens, and the only barrier which now interposes between the liberties of the people and the consolidating power of a centralized despotism at Washington is the sovereignty of the State.

Let not the willing tools of the recently initiated tyranny in this country imagine that the Press is to be deterred by the threats contained in this unconstitutional law against all who interfere with its operation. We have too much faith in the Executive of the Empire State to suppose that he will ever allow an Administration which is sapping the very foundations of constitutional freedom to seize upon his fellow-citizens as the Russian autocrat has attempted to do with the ill-fated victims of his fiendish rule in Poland. The moment such an assault is made upon citizen rights, the last links that bind the States together will be rent asunder like so many cobwebs. The Administration will then find, when it is too late, that it is the States which constitute the Republic, that they are sovereign, that it is the powers which they have delegated that make up what is called the General Government, that they are as the pillars which support a grand dome, and that the moment their support is withdrawn, that part of the edifice must fall to the ground.

Of course the enforcement of such an act, with all the rigors of the despotic power for the furtherance of whose policy it was concocted, could not be accomplished without providing for the punishment of all offending against its provisions. This was fully understood by the men who framed this most tyrannical of all the tyrannical acts of that notoriously tyrannical body—the last Congress; and so they inserted the following impotent threat:

SEC. 25. *And be it further enacted,* That if any person shall resist any draft of men enrolled under this act into the service of the United States, or shall counsel or aid any person to resist any such draft; or shall assault or obstruct any officer in making such draft, or in the performance of any service in relation thereto; or shall counsel any person to assault or obstruct any such officer, or shall counsel any drafted men not to appear at the place of rendezvous, *or willfully dissuade them from the performance of military duty as required by law, such person shall be subject to summary arrest by the provost marshal, and shall be forthwith delivered to the civil authorities, and, upon conviction thereof, be punished by a fine not exceeding five hundred dollars, or by imprisonment not exceeding two years, or by both of said punishments.*

If this were really a war for the Constitution and the Union, and not for the military subjugation of a portion of our fellow-countrymen, there would be no occasion for a conscription; but we tell the Chief Executive at Washington that the conscription will fail, miserably fail, and that its failure will be produced by the very influences evoked by his emancipation policy, and his other unconstitutional acts.

We do not think so meanly of the American people, despite of their long patience and forbearance, as to imagine that they are yet ready to tolerate a military despotism; neither do we believe that they are in favor of the still further prosecution of this war, to carry out the designs of a radical Abolition minority. For our own part, we never could convince ourselves that the Union would ever be restored through such an ordeal. We always regarded it as a union of free-will and not of force; and we have never entertained any other belief than that which we now express, when we say that the sword will inevitably prove the cause of its disintegration.

That the Conscription Act is unconstitutional is evident from a perusal of its provisions; but the manner of its passage is no less unconstitutional. If the reports of the closing hours of Congress be correct, it was carried in the Senate by a trick, a vile fraud upon the people. This is apparent in the following extract which we make from the report:

Mr. Powell spoke until half-past three o'clock in the morning, when he moved that the Senate adjourn.

Motion rejected by yeas 4, nays 32.

Mr. Bayard commenced speaking against the bill, and spoke until half-past four o'clock, when he *yielded the floor to Mr. Powell*, who again moved that the House adjourn.

Motion rejected by yeas 4, nays 33.

The question then recurred on agreeing *to the report of the Conference Committee.*

The vote was called, and the Chairman, Mr. Pomeroy, *declared the report agreed to.*

Mr. Trumbull moved to take up the act relative to the validity of the deeds of public squares to the city of Washington.

Motion agreed to.

Mr. Powell—I hope that the Senate will proceed with *the consideration of the report of the Conference Committee.*

Mr. Grimes—THAT BILL IS PASSED.

Mr. Powell—Oh, no! The Senator from Delaware (Bayard) is entitled to the floor.

Mr. Trumbull—*I call the Senator from Kentucky* (Powell) *to order. I am on the floor, and I moved to take up another bill, and that motion has been carried.*

Mr. Bayard—Neither the manner nor the language of the Senator from Illinois (Trumbull) will cause me *to yield my right to the floor, to which I am entitled.*

Mr. Powell—Do I understand the Chairman (Pomeroy) to say that the bill is passed?

The Chair—*The bill is passed.*

Mr. Powell—By what kind of jockeying?

Mr. Trumbull—I call the Senator from Kentucky to order.

Mr. Bayard—Does the Chair decide the report of the Conference Committee to have been adopted by any vote of the Senate?

The Chair—I UNDERSTAND *that the report has been adopted.*

Mr. Powell—Did I not most distinctly state that the Senator from Delaware (Bayard) *only yielded the floor to a motion to adjourn?*

The Chair—*I did not hear the Senator from Kentucky say that the Senator from Delaware yielded the floor for any particular purpose.*

Mr. Trumbull—I believe that I am entitled to the floor.

The Chair—*The Senator from Illinois* (Trumbull) *is entitled to the floor unless he yields it.*

Mr. Powell—I desire to ask the Chair——

Mr. Trumbull—*I do not yield to the Senator from Kentucky to ask any question.*

Mr. Bayard—I desire to appeal from the decision of the Chair. *I desire to ascertain whether the minority have any rights remaining here.*

Mr. Howard moved that the Senate adjourn.

Mr. Richardson moved to reconsider the motion by which the bill was claimed to be passed by the Senate.

Mr. Grimes—Did the Senator from Illinois (Richardson) vote with the majority? If he did not, he could not move for a reconsideration.

At a quarter to five A.M. the Senate adjourned.

It appears from the foregoing that Mr. Bayard, after speaking at some length against the bill, yielded the floor to a motion of adjournment made by Mr. Powell, as such motions are always in order. In the event of the rejection of the motion, the right to the floor reverted to Mr. Bayard according to the rules of debate. But before Mr. Bayard could resume the right which he had only temporarily yielded, a vote was taken on the bill as reported by the Conference Committee, and the Chairman declared its adoption. Such a nefarious transaction was never perpetrated upon the liberties of a people, if we except that by which the nationality of Ireland was filched away by a corrupt legislature, acting under the direction of a man whose name will be infamous throughout all coming time, and whose death was a fitting termination to a life of the blackest crime.

Never had a legislative body such a glorious opportunity of saving the life of a nation and the liberties of a people, as that which the last Congress was presented; but instead of using its power and its influence in the form of mild and conciliatory measures to win back the love of the Southern people to the Union, it did all in its power to render the very name of Union hateful to them by the adoption of a policy which has resulted in uniting the whole South in one compact confederacy, with a thoroughly organized Government, with an army whose bravery and heroism can not be doubted, and with statesmen at its head to whom the petty politicians at Washington are pigmies in comparison. The people do not forget that it was through the compulsory influence exercised by this Congress upon the Administration, that General McClellan was removed, and it was also through its sectional and abolition legislation that a wide-spread discontent has been created in the Union army. They know, also, that it was in compliance with its demands the President issued his last proclamation, and we think they are by this time convinced that they will be satisfied with no other submission on the part of the South than that which would lay her prostrate and bleeding at the feet of the newly-created American despot. If this is the union in which this war is to terminate, then farewell to the liberty of the people. The once free, happy, and prosperous nation known as the United States will pass away as did the republics of ancient Greece—flashing like a meteor across the sky of time, and lighting up with a dazzling brilliancy the surrounding nations that gazed with wonder on the startling phenomenon. Is this really to be the fate of the great Republic? The people alone can answer that question, and upon their answer depends the future destiny of the New World.

We know there are men in our midst, for we lately had disgraceful evidence of the fact, who would aid the newly constituted tyranny at Washington in riveting its fetters upon the people. Such men assume to be the mouthpieces of the conservative masses, but they will find, when too late, that the trickery of the demagogue to which they have resorted will not save them from the judgment of an incensed and outraged people. Such men may imagine that the liberty of a nation is a thing of trifling value; but as long as the great heart of the people is right, their intrigues in the interest of American autocracy will prove a wretched failure. These are the energies against which the great statesmen of the Republic have warned us again and again; it is they who are ready to assist in undoing the work of the patriots of the Revolution by ignoring the Constitution, and handing over the rights of the people to a military dictator to put under bolt and bar. Such men can see no harm in the suspension of the habeas corpus, in the suppression of the liberty of the press, in the overthrow of State sovereignty, in the arbitrary arrest and incarceration in government dungeons of loyal citizens, in proclamations placing loyal and sovereign States under martial law, and in investing the so-called President of the United States with supreme power above the Constitution, above State rights, above all law, over the personal liberty of the citizen. Such things, in their estimation, are a mere bagatelle. The liberty for which the infant Republic waged a seven-years' war against Great Britain is to be bartered away, and for what? A military despotism—not even such a despotism as they have in some parts of Europe—but a despotism directed by men who have proved themselves weak in everything else but the will to destroy. They are ready to carry out the conscription; but so long as they are the owners of three hundred dollars, not one of them, we venture to say, will take the field. They will leave that for the poor man, whose family is dependent upon him for support. They are the heroes of the rostrum, and not of the battle-field, whose dangers they are satisfied to view at a safe distance. They are the men who will "look into Catholicity when slavery is disposed of," for to them religious freedom is of still less importance than civil rights.

But they must be blind to the evidence, which is growing stronger day by day, that the people are opposed to a war waged for emancipation—to a war which, if successful in that object, will flood the labor markets of the North with black competitors against the interests of the white industrial classes, or dot our Northern land with poor-houses for the support of an indigent negro population either unwilling or unable to work.

Despite of all this, however, their voice is still for war, but while they talk of the carnage of the battle *they act peace.* They urge others into the field, but *they* are content to stay at home that they may add new force to the blow that is aimed at the liberty of the people. They accuse the advocates of peace with treason, while *they act treason by declining to fight.* They can see no danger to popular liberty by intrusting the President with supreme control over the sword and purse of the nation. They approve the act of Congress by which nearly two billion three hundred millions of dollars are put at the disposal of the Chief Executive—a sum more than half the national debt of England. *Do they expect to be paid a portion of it for their support of a centralized despotism?*

In this State, however, we need have no fear of the result, so far as the rights of the citizen are concerned, for we have a Chief Magistrate who has pledged himself to their defense and support, and whose inaugural message contains the following solemn guarantee against the encroachments of arbitrary power:

> While our soldiers (says he) are periling their lives to uphold the Constitution and to restore the Union, we owe to them who have shown an endurance and patriotism unsurpassed in the history of the world, that we emulate their devotion in our field of duty. We are to take care, when they come back, that their home rights are not impaired, that they shall not find when they return to the duties of civil life that the SECURITY OF THEIR PERSONS, THE SANCTITY OF THEIR HOMES, OR THE PROTECTION OF THEIR PROPERTY have been lost by us while they were battling for the national interest in a distant field of duty.

The following extracts from the same important document are particularly applicable at the present time, and in view of the unconstitutional course of Congress, and the violation of the supreme law of the land by the so-called President, we submit them to the consideration of our readers:

> The rights of States were reserved, and the powers of the General Government were limited *to protect the people in their persons, property, and consciences in times of danger and civil commotion.* There is little to fear in

periods of peace and prosperity. If we are not protected when there are popular excitements and convulsions, *our government is a failure. If presidential proclamations are above the decisions of the courts and the restraints of the Constitution, then that Constitution is a mockery. If it has not the authority to keep the Executive within its restraints, then it can not retain States within the Union. Those who hold that there is no sanctity in the Constitution must equally hold that there is no guilt in the rebellion.*

We can not be silent and allow these practices to become precedents. They are as much in violation of our Constitution as the rebellion itself, and more dangerous to our liberties. They hold out to the Executive every temptation of ambition to make and prolong war. They offer despotic power as a price for preventing peace. They are inducements to each administration to procure discord and incite armed resistance to law, by declaring that the condition of war removes all constitutional restraints. They call about the national capital hordes of unprincipled men, who find in the wreck of their country the opportunity to gratify avarice and ambition, or personal or political resentments. This theory makes the passion and ambition of an administration antagonistic to the interest and happiness of the people. It makes the restoration of peace the abdication of more than regal authority in the hands of those to whom is confided the government of the country.

After perusing the foregoing, our readers will, we think, agree with us that liberty of speech and of the press are secure under a Governor who appreciates his position and is determined to maintain the sovereignty of the great State at the head of which he has been placed, *not by a minority*, but by *a majority* of its citizens. We believe that our right as a journalist to utter, and print, and circulate freely and without danger of arbitrary arrest and incarceration, whatever we find to criticise in the acts of the Administration—we believe that our right to do this will be maintained by the Chief Executive of the Empire State, and it is in this belief that we now exercise that *Constitutional right*, despite of the threats of a military despotism, and its base and venal adherents.

If the people are not fully aroused to the dangers by which their liberties, not to speak of their sovereignty, are beset, they may soon lose both the opportunity and the power to preserve those priceless boons for which such great sacrifices were made.

CAN A DISUNION ADMINISTRATION RESTORE THE UNION?

FACTS THAT CAN NOT BE CONTROVERTED, AND THAT EVERY AMERICAN SHOULD KNOW AND UNDERSTAND.

(*From the* METROPOLITAN RECORD *of March* 28, 1863.)

WE believe that all unbiased and candid minds will agree with us, that the Union might and could have been restored by any other Administration than that whose term of service will unfortunately not expire for two years longer, but whose exit from office would be the greatest benefit that could be conferred upon the country. We are aware that this assertion will be combated most vigorously by those who sustain and advocate the policy of the so-called national Administration; but we shall appeal to their sense of impartiality and justice while we present for their consideration a few facts and observations on the course which it has pursued since the commencement of our present fratricidal, unnecessary, inhuman, and abolition war.

Our jocular and anecdotal Chief Magistrate, in that extraordinary advance of his from Springfield to Washington two years ago, made quite a number of humorous little speeches, in one of which he pleasantly informed the public that "nobody was hurt."

His *entrée* into Washington, it will be remembered, was made in disguise—a Scotch cap and military cloak being used on the occasion for the better concealment of the newly-elected magistrate of the great Republic. It was a mean disguise, unworthy of the Executive of a free people; it was like the manner in which Kossuth left this country, under a false exterior.

This was a bad beginning; slight as the incident may appear, it wore a bad aspect. Why should the President of thirty millions of freemen slink into the capital of the country in a manner that was calculated only to excite contempt and ridicule? Why did he not boldly and fearlessly proceed on his journey as if he had nothing to dread from his fellow-citizens—as if he had a full reliance on their sense of right and justice? If he intended to act in accordance with the Constitution—if he intended to deal impartially between the North and the South—if he did not design to force upon the country the peculiar policy of the minority by which he was elected, why did he not boldly, and frankly, and manfully enter the capital of the nation?

Ah! that beginning, without significance as it may appear in the eyes of some, was painfully suggestive to all who desired the future happiness, prosperity, and freedom of the country.

Such was the advent of Mr. Lincoln into Washington—a city where his illustrious predecessors in office were in the habit of appearieg in public unattended except by admiring friends, but where he the latest (and we hope not the last) President seldom makes his appearance in public except under the protection of an armed guard.

His inaugural informed the country that he would conduct the affairs of the Government on national principles—that he would not interfere with the peculiar institution of the South. "Apprehension," said he, "seems to exist among the people in the Southern States that, by the accession of a Republican Administration, their property and their peace and personal security are to be endangered. * * * * I do but quote from one of my speeches when I declare that I have no purpose, directly or indirectly, to interfere with the institution of slavery in the States where it exists. *I believe I have no lawful right to do so, and I have no inclination to do so.*"

This is pretty plain; there is no misunderstanding its meaning, that is if words have not changed their signification. Mr. Lincoln then said that he had no intention to interfere with the institution of Slavery; but how have his subsequent acts redeemed his promise to the people? Did he give any encouragement to the objects of the Border State Convention? Did not the party by which he was supported and placed in office refuse to agree to any terms of conciliation or compromise with the South? Did they not treat with scorn and contempt the policy of the greatest statesmen of the country who knew and who stated again and again that the Republic could never be held together except governed by the spirit of mutual concession and forbearance? Were they not aware that the Constitution itself was a compromise? and were they so blind as not to see that a President elected on the principle of geographical distinctions and sectional considerations must pursue a thoroughly constitutional and national course if he would preserve the integrity of the nation? All this was patent to the most superficial observer, and yet with all this knowledge in their possession—with all these self-evident facts before them—they have pursued a course at once subversive of the Constitution under which they have pretended to act, and ruinous to the interests of the great nation which they so falsely claim to represent. It was through their machinations that the objects of the Border State Convention were defeated. They were such firm and fast adherents to abolition principles, that they would not compromise with slavery, although no men knew better than they that the immortal Washington himself was a slaveholder. With a pharisaical assumption of superior moral excellence, they haughtily declined to make any compromise with their Southern fellow-citizens; and in their acts, if not in their words, they scouted the memory and the truly national policy of the great man who had in his day saved the country through such conciliatory measures. What more did the leaders at the South require than this—than the proof thus afforded—that the party which supported the Administration was inimical to everything that looked to a friendly adjustment of the great questions in controversy? What, let us ask, could the North lose by compromising with the South? Was she asked to give up any of her rights? Was any material injury to be inflicted thereby upon Northern interests? Certainly not. In giving to the South all that section demanded, we should only yield that to which she was justly entitled. What, then, was the great obstacle in the way of compromise? "*Principle!*" The Northern representatives at the Border State Convention were actuated solely by their adherence to principle! If it were not for the terrible tragedy which has formed the historical sequel to that Convention, this pretension to principle might be laughed at as farcical. But there is blood on their hands, and the dread and horrible picture of tens of thousands slain upon the gory battle-field, and of the myriads of sad, weeping mourners in Northern and Southern homes, who shall look in vain for the beloved ones that will never more return—all those should haunt their imaginations, if they have heads to think and hearts to feel. They had a glorious and noble opportunity to save their country; but like an inhuman and unnatural parricide who flings his father into the foaming torrent, they made no effort to escue it from destruction.

The Border State Convention was "a mockery, a delusion, and a snare," and the majority of the men who went there from the Northern States did so with the determination to oppose every measure that was calculated to re-establish friendly relations between the two great sections of the country. It might have saved the Republic, but it failed, miserably, ignominiously failed.

What was their next step? The war having commenced with the attack on Fort Sumter—which was nothing more nor less than the culmination of Northern abolitionism and John Brownism—a requisition was made upon the country for *seventy-five thousand* men with which to put down about one third of the population, and to accomplish this in the remarkably brief period of three months. The Government issued a political promissory note payable in ninety days, in the shape of a submissive and repentant South, and one of its cabinet officers indorsed the paper to render it acceptable to the shrewd money-lenders of the country. Unfortunately, however, the promise to pay was not redeemed. The end of the three months beheld the South more defiant and less submissive than at the commencement, and so a further extension of time was required. Three months more were necessary, and the country, again deluded, once more yielded. The six months flew by—the seventy-five thousand men were increased to five hundred thousand, and the Congress which has so fearfully misrepresented the people voted five hundred millions of dollars—for what? The abolition of slavery and the overthrow of State rights. The five hundred thousand men and the five hundred millions of dollars "have gone in the wind." The country is more divided than ever. The South has assumed the form of a compact nationality, and the confidence of the loyal people of the North has been so far betrayed and imposed upon by the men who have ruled only to ruin, that they have lost all trust in, and have long since learned to look upon, the authorities at Washington only with contempt and distrust. What followed the immense outpouring of the people into the ranks of the volunteer army? Nothing but defeat and disaster. That grand army was broken up and scattered in detachments along the line of the war; it was defeated at several points; but the greatest disaster of all befell it close by the capital of Virginia, and subsequently in the near vicinity of Washington. The South was a unit in its opposition to the ill-judged invasion from the North. Its people had been forced into a unanimity of feeling by the abolition legislation of a sectional Congress. That Congress, with an inhuman disregard to the lives of the brave men who believed they were fighting for the whole country and not for the success of the principles of a party, was engaged meanwhile in the enactment of laws inimical to the interests of the South, and calculated only to provoke the most embittered feelings of sectional animosity and hatred. It passed a bill for the emancipation of slaves in the District of Columbia, although there were not more than two thousand of them in that section. This, we do not hesitate to say, was, considering its result, the most atrocious and the most ruinous legislative act that could have been adopted in the then condition of the country. It revealed the animus of the men who had got into power; it created dismay in the ranks of the conservative men who sincerely loved their country and who had been flattered by the vain hope that Congress would not push its sectional policy to an extreme degree.

But what was the course of the Administration during this period? What return did it make to the loyal North for the immense army and vast sums of money which had been placed at its disposal? What return did it make for all this? Let us enumerate: Freedom of speech and of the Press placed under censorship; the arbitrary arrest and incarceration of loyal citizens; the conversion of forts, which were intended for defense against invasion by a foreign foe, into bastiles for the imprisonment of freemen; the overthrow of State rights, and the breaking down of State boundaries; the flagrant and unnecessary violation of constitutional guarantees; the fiendish frauds practiced upon men who volunteered for the defense of the Union and the Constitution, but who had been sacrificed to Abolition designs. These are some of the returns which have been made by the Administration to the people for the trust and confidence which was so freely given, but which has been so vilely abused.

Having failed, even through the aid of a draft which increased our army to eight or nine hundred thousand men, to bring back the South, the President resorted, in the last extremity, to his Emancipation Proclamation, threatening the seceded States with all the horrors of a negro insurrection in the event of their continued obstinacy. It was a desperate expedient, and could have its conception only in the brains or the perverted imagination of an Abolition fanatic.

It declared the slaves of all the States in rebellion free after a hundred days; but his declaration of freedom has had no more effect on them than that mythical "bull against the comet," which, with the jocularity that characterizes even his most serious moments, he compared it with.

But this was not all; for that "bull" which he issued against the South has only returned *to gore its owner*. It was not enough, however, that he should increase the bitter feeling in the South, he must also insult the loyal North by placing it under martial law, and annulling, thereby, the supreme law of the land. We say that this was not only an insult, but it was worse; it was the subjection of Northern citizens to military authority; it was the overthrow of State rights, and the beginning of a system of consolidation which, if permitted by the people, must inevitably result in the establishment of a permanent military despotism.

We ask any candid reader if, in the foregoing review, we have not presented a truthful statement of the policy of the Administration and its ruinous effects upon the present condition and future prospects of the country. Is it possible, after the sad experience of the past two years, that any man can believe the present war will result in the restoration of the Union? Are we not farther from this consummation than we were two years ago? Have we not in the Administration the same tools to work with that we have been using so ineffectually during that period? Has not that Administration been furnished at various times with armies amounting in the aggregate to fifteen hundred thousand men, and with the sinews of war to the amount of one thousand millions of dollars? What proof have we that another thousand millions of dollars will not be as recklessly squandered, and another fifteen hundred thousand men as fruitlessly employed in binding together with the sword the severed members of a broken Union? Has the Administration not furnished us with sufficient evidence of its own incompetency, and the utter impracticability of the desperate undertaking in which it has so recklessly engaged? For we insist that *the work of subjugating the South is an impossibility;* and when the Administration called in the aid of negro slaves by a vile and infamous proclamation, a proclamation that should make the blood of every freeman tingle in his veins, that should mantle the temple of every American citizen with the crimson blush of shame—when the Administration did this, it afforded to the world an admission of its impossibility. What a disgraceful avowal was contained in the bill presented in Congress for the enlistment of three hundred thousand negroes! What a fiendish expedient with which to make war upon the defenseless women and children of the South, and to rouse against the Republic the indignation of civilized humanity! Did those recreants to their own race think of their wives and children as they sat brooding in demoniac council over the fiendish plot that was to bring massacre, and rapine, and outrage into the homes on Southern plantations, sprinkling their hearths with the blood of gentle women, helpless age, and innocent childhood? Never was a blacker crime sought to be committed against nature, against humanity, against the holy precepts of Christianity, and against all principles of manly and civilized warfare. There is no language sufficiently strong to brand this diabolical measure as it deserves. But it will fail, as it has failed already in the first instance, and as we trust for the honor of the country, for the honor of the American name, for the honor of our common humanity which has been outraged in its best instincts, we trust such measures will always and ever fail.

This may be construed as treason; but we are utterly indifferent to the charge. We have not yet learned to speak of the powers that be with bated breath and whispering humbleness. We are, as we have ever been, opposed to this war. We are for peace, and to secure this end we are in favor of an armistice. We have had two years of war without any result, so far as the restoration of the Union is concerned. Let us try peace, and a Convention of the States. We have had enough of blood, and only the cormorants that surround the White House, and that are to be found in the purlieus of the Capitol fattening on the public treasury, growing rich as the country grows poor, heaping up their ill-gotten gains which augment with the increase of taxes that are already crushing down the industrial classes of the country; only such as these will oppose the demand. The man who insists upon the prolongation of this war *should do that which he wants others to do;* he should not wait for the conscription; he should shoulder his musket and march to the battle-field, where the deadly rifle-ball is the only argument with which he will have to deal.

Yes, this work of blood has gone on long enough, and it is time to understand the lesson which we have been taught by the last two years—*that the military subjugation of the South is an impossibility.* We are told that anything is preferable to a divided country, but a Union under a military despotism would be still worse. *Besides, how is it possible that the representatives of a party which has been actuated and governed by the spirit of division and disunion from its very inception can restore the Union?*

Are figs of thistles,
Or grapes of thorns?

Has not the Abolition party been the party of disunion, and has not the President adopted their policy in his Emancipation Proclamation? The Abolitionists are to this country what the Orangemen are to Ireland. They feed and live upon dissension. For our own part, we have no hope of union from the present Administration, and the sooner, therefore, this war stops, the better it will be for the people and the preservation of their liberties. Let us be warned in time; let us be no longer deceived. We must depend for our protection upon the Sovereign States; they are the breakwater upon which the encroaching waves of Federal usurpation will break in vain. Let us not abandon the principle of freedom for a Union which would be unprofitable without it. There is a union between England and Ireland. There is a union between Russia and Poland. *In both instances the union has been accomplished and maintained by the sword.* Is that the union we seek? Is the South to be a dependency held by the military power of the North, which, to secure the connection, must give up its liberties and merge its State sovereignties into a consolidated despotism.

Let us, then, have peace. Let the people tell the Administration there has been enough of blood-letting, and that its creatures have had enough of plunder from the public treasury. Let the attempt to enforce the Conscription Act be met with the demand for peace—a demand which, swelling up in thunder tones from the great heart of the people, will warn the Administration that its disunion policy is at an end, that the war must cease, and that, through the instrumentality of a National Convention, to be called by the Sovereign States, they will meet their brethren of the South, as freemen should meet freemen, in the spirit of compromise and conciliation. If the Union is ever to be restored, it will be through such means, and such means alone; but if the policy of the Administration has rendered reunion impossible, then let us preserve our liberty, and let us see to it that the precious gift bequeathed to us by the freemen of the Revolution is not lost through the supineness and indifference of their unworthy descendants, who, in grasping at the shadow, have lost the substance.

A GREAT STATESMAN SPEAKING TO THE PEOPLE.

ALEXANDER HAMILTON ON COERCION AND CIVIL WAR.

(*From the* METROPOLITAN RECORD, *April* 4, 1863.)

THE following is an extract from a speech, delivered in 1788, of that great statesman and true patriot, Alexander Hamilton, in the Convention that was held in the State of New York for the ratification of the Constitution of the United States. It will be remembered that Hamilton was also a member of the Convention which framed the Constitution:

"THE STATES CAN NEVER LOSE THEIR POWERS TILL THE WHOLE PEOPLE OF AMERICA ARE ROBBED OF THEIR LIBERTIES. THESE MUST GO TOGETHER. THEY MUST SUPPORT EACH OTHER OR MEET A COMMON FATE. I WISH THE COMMITTEE TO REMEMBER THAT THE CONSTITUTION UNDER EXAMINATION IS FRAMED UPON TRULY REPUBLICAN PRINCIPLES, AND THAT, AS IT IS EXPRESSLY DESIGNED FOR A COMMON PROTECTION AND THE GENERAL WELFARE OF THE UNITED STATES, IT MUST BE UTTERLY REPUGNANT TO THIS CONSTITUTION TO SUBVERT THE STATE GOVERNMENTS OR OPPRESS THE PEOPLE. THE COERCION OF STATES IS ONE OF THE MADDEST PROJECTS THAT WAS EVER DEVISED. A FAILURE OF COMPLIANCE WILL NEVER BE CONFINED TO A SINGLE STATE. THIS BEING THE CASE, CAN WE SUPPOSE IT WISE TO HAZARD A CIVIL WAR? IT WOULD BE A NATION AT WAR WITH ITSELF. CAN ANY REASONABLE MAN BE WELL DISPOSED TOWARD A GOVERNMENT THAT MAKES WAR AND CARNAGE THE ONLY MEANS OF SUPPORTING ITSELF—A GOVERNMENT THAT CAN EXIST ONLY BY THE SWORD? EVERY SUCH WAR MUST INVOLVE THE INNOCENT WITH THE GUILTY. THIS SINGLE CONSIDERATION SHOULD NOT BE INEFFICIENT TO DISPOSE EVERY PEACEABLE CITIZEN AGAINST SUCH A GOVERNMENT."

We have given more than usual prominence to this extract from the patriotic speech of one of the greatest statesmen of the Revolution—a man who was justly regarded by Washington with the highest esteem, and who was considered by some writers as one of the first among the patriots of that period. Never was such a warning more needed than at the present time, when the people are apparently so indifferent to the daily encroachments of a sectional administration upon their rights and liberties Our present troubles are mainly owing to the frequent departures which have been witnessed in these days from the principles of the Revolution, and we shall never restore the integrity of the country until we return to the position maintained through every emergency by the fathers of the Republic.

Hamilton said that the Constitution was expressly designed for the common protection and the general welfare of the United States; but what protection has it afforded to the citizen against arbitrary arrest—against the suppression of freedom of speech and of the press, against the overthrow of State sovereignty, against the suspension of the habeas corpus, against the seizure of the very judge upon the bench?—what protection has it afforded under all these circumstances? Absolutely none. Abraham Lincoln—a man who is as immeasurably below Alexander Hamilton as the black race is below the white—has found in his sectional policy a pretext for setting aside that Constitution which Hamilton told us is expressly designed for the common protection and the general welfare of the United States. He has not found it "repugnant" thereto to subvert the State governments, or oppress the people; and he evidently does not consider that "the coercion of States is one of the maddest of projects that was ever devised." Neither does he regard it as unwise to hazard a civil war; and as for the fact of it being "a nation at war with itself," what matters it so long as the wretched creatures who are waxing fat upon the miseries of the people can heap up their ill-gotten wealth.

Let those who would prolong this war, and who would denounce us for our opposition to the course of the Administration, read the startling words of Alexander Hamilton. Our reply to their denunciation will be found in the following sentence, which is particularly appropriate, and possesses a peculiar significance at the present time:

"CAN ANY REASONABLE MAN BE WELL DISPOSED TOWARD A GOVERNMENT THAT MAKES WAR AND CARNAGE THE ONLY MEANS OF SUPPORTING ITSELF—A GOVERNMENT THAT CAN EXIST ONLY BY THE SWORD?"

Let us ask if this so-called national Administration does not make "war and carnage the only means of supporting itself?" Does not it and its creatures threaten every man that dares to advocate a discontinuance of the war? and has not Congress placed the purse and *sword* of the nation under its complete control? The single consideration alluded to by Hamilton has disposed ourselves as well as "every peaceable citizen against such a Government."

But we have other reasons equally powerful in favor of a discontinuance of the war. We entertain serious fears for the perpetuation of popular liberty. We behold growing up day by day a constantly increasing class, who find their interest in the present fratricidal conflict. We see springing up a so-called *Loyal* League, which, if not crushed out by public opinion, may be employed as a garrison in every city and town and village in the land, to tyrannize over the people, and to keep them down, as the Poles have been kept down by Russia, by the strong arm of despotic force. When we realize the immense moneyed power and influence in the control of the President, we fear for the future freedom of the people—that is, if the people are untrue to themselves. We fear that political corruption, through the ever-ready bribe of place or profit, may undermine the official integrity of our representatives in Congress, and render them the ready and willing tools of a debased and demoralized Administration. Let the people be warned in time. Let them assemble in mass meetings all over the country, and convey, through such mediums, their desires and their demands to their representatives. It is true that we will have a conservative majority in the next Congress; but let us take care that our representatives are not bought, as it is said was done with one of the members of our State Legislature. A shrewd but corrupt statesman once said that every man had his price. If this be so, let us ascertain how much it would cost the Administration to secure the vote of any purchasable member for the support of its Abolition policy. If by the expenditure of four or five millions of its eight millions *secret fund* it could buy a sufficient number of votes to give it a majority in Congress, what security would the people have against the establishment of a permanent military despotism—what security save through a successful and bloody revolution?

If the people are indifferent to their future rights and

liberties—if they are ready to yield the precious inheritance bequeathed to them by the patriots of the Revolution—then, indeed, it is a matter of utter indifference how their representatives may act in the next vital and important session of Congress. But if they would preserve their freedom and independence intact, they will, as we have said, assemble in mass meetings throughout the country, and instruct their representatives in such a manner as to leave no doubt whatever in regard to the course they are to pursue.

We sincerely trust that the next Congress will not adjourn until it shall have presented a bill of impeachment against the President for his repeated and flagrant violations of the Constitution.

We punish the burglar who enters our house at the dead hour of night and carries away our property. Why, then, should we allow the highest public official in the land, the chief servant of the people, who has stolen our liberties, or attempted to do so—why should we allow him to escape? We inflict the severest penalty known to the law upon him who takes the life of his fellow-man. Shall the man whose policy has aimed a deadly blow at the national life escape the penalties imposed by the Constitution?

GROUNDS OF IMPEACHMENT OF THE PRESIDENT.

(*From the* METROPOLITAN RECORD, *April* 11, 1863.)

THAT there are grounds for impeachment no one who has watched the course of the Executive can doubt. If the Constitution were so much waste paper, it could not have been more contemptuously thrown aside. Every provision which tended to secure individual liberty has been set at naught; the barriers which it erected against Federal usurpation have been trampled under foot; and the President of the United States possesses at the present moment as much power as the Autocrat of all the Russias. *Possesses!* but will hardly dare to use; for men born to freedom and brought up in the exercise of citizen rights, can not with impunity be treated as serfs or even as subjects. The pliant Congress that manufactured a Dictator out of a Republican President made but sorry work of it when it omitted to transform citizens into slaves. The edifice of despotism, like every other edifice, is subject to architectural laws, and must be built *up*, not *down*. To be successful, they should have begun with the people, not the President. The people are still true to Republican principles, they love the Government which their fathers founded, they cling to the Constitution even as the shipwrecked mariner clings to his last chance of safety, and they glory in that majestic aggregate of free federated republics which we call the Union. The great heart of the people is sound at the core, as evidenced in the overwhelming conservative majorities returned against the Administration candidates in New York, Ohio, Illinois, Indiana, Pennsylvania, and New Jersey. The men thus returned are a living protest against the Administration—they are the embodied rebuke of six sovereign States against the policy which has thus far governed the Chief Executive. These political victories prove the radical change that has taken place in public opinion since the previous elections; they indicate that the tide is on the turn whose refluent waves will sweep away the knaves and fools and fanatics who have brought disgrace upon our proud Republic. These victories are the death-knell of the Abolition party, and they must strike upon the Presidential ear like an alarm-bell in the night.

Men returned upon this express issue of opposition to the Administration will not shrink from impeaching the President whenever it is deemed expedient to do so. Let us enumerate some of the grounds on which he is open to impeachment. The Constitution says:

> Article 4. The right of the people to be secure in their persons, houses, papers, and effects, against unreasonable searches and seizures, shall not be violated. And no warrant shall issue but upon probable causes, supported by oath or affirmation, and particularly describing the place to be searched, and the person or thing to be seized.

We will not insult our readers by proving that this article has been violated.

The Constitution says:

Art. 5. No person shall be held to answer for a capital, or otherwise infamous crime, unless on a presentment or indictment of a grand jury, except in cases arising in the land or naval forces, or in the militia, when in actual service in time of war or danger; . . . . . nor be deprived of life, liberty, or property, without due process of law.

And this article has been violated.

The Constitution says:

Art. 1, sec. 2. When vacancies happen in the representation from any State, the executive authority thereof shall issue writs of election to fill such vacancies.

And this has been violated.

The Constitution says:

Art. 1, sec. 9. The privilege of the writ of habeas corpus shall not be suspended, unless when, in cases of rebellion or invasion, the public safety may require it.

And this has been again and again outrageously and flagrantly violated.

The Constitution says:

Art. 3, sec. 3. Treason against the United States shall consist only in levying war against them, or in adhering to their enemies, giving them aid and comfort. No person shall be convicted of treason unless on the testimony of two witnesses to the same overt act, or on confession in open court.

The very walls of the Government bastiles could testify to the violation of this article.

Under the same article and section we find that Congress has power to declare the punishment of treason; but mark what follows:

No attainder of treason shall work corruption of blood, or forfeiture, except during the life of the person attainted.

Call to mind the emancipation proclamation, declaring negroes henceforth and forever free; and also the Confiscation Act, which is a gross violation of the Constitution.

The Constitution says:

Art. 4, sec. 3. No new State shall be formed or erected within the jurisdiction of any other State . . . . without the consent of the Legislature of the State concerned as well as of the Congress.

Is not Kanawha an ever-present proof of a violated Constitution?

We come now to other articles of the Constitution, and we find the express declaration:

> Congress shall make no law . . . . abridging the freedom of speech or of the press.

The suspension of conservative papers and the incarceration of outspoken men testifies, trumpet-tongued, to the violation of this fundamental right of freemen.

The Constitution says:

> Art. 2. The right of the people to keep and bear arms shall not be infringed.

This has also been violated.

Here, then, is matter for impeachment—here are express violations of the Constitution. But there are others not less serious, concerning which the Constitution is silent, and which are in direct opposition to the essence and spirit of that immortal document. The Constitution does not say expressly there must be no espionage exercised by Government over the citizens of the Republic. Military governors must not be appointed, test oaths, illegal and arbitrary, must not be prescribed, martial law must not be proclaimed over States not in rebellion, white men must not be taxed to purchase freedom for the negro; but these things were not forbidden, simply because they were not foreseen. Who doubts that they are in direct opposition to the spirit of the Constitution? If violations of the letter and spirit of the Constitution can be compassed with impunity, and that, too, by men bound by solemn obligations to support it—men who owe their continuance in office to the very instrument they violate—if such criminals 'scape "unwhipt of justice," then adieu to Liberty, and "farewell, a long farewell to all our greatness."

The impeachment of Abraham Lincoln would vindicate the majesty of the Constitution, and to the next Congress we look for that vindication. We shall conclude by giving the solemn oath which he took on the day of his inauguration:

> *I do solemnly swear (or affirm) that I will faithfully execute the office of President of the United States, and will, to the best of my ability, preserve, protect, and defend the Constitution of the United States.*

How has this oath been kept?

THE EFFECTS OF ABOLITIONISM.

(*From the* METROPOLITAN RECORD, *April* 4, 1863.)

THE American people, with all their shrewdness, with all their business tact, with all their so-called Yankee 'cuteness, which is said always to get the best in a bargain, are the most easily humbugged in the world. They have not only tolerated, but, to a great extent, nurtured and sustained a party that has caused a division of the country, and that, if longer sustained and tolerated, will plunge it into irremediable anarchy and ruin.

Never was a nation so afflicted, so cursed by a miserable faction in its midst, a faction which has lived upon discord, and the triumph of which has been the knell of the Republic. It has been the unswerving ally of a foreign foe, and it has worked with a zeal that knew no ceasing to overthrow the liberties of a nation which was based upon the principles of self-government. Claiming to work in the interests of humanity, it has plunged the land in a civil war, that has rocked it to and fro as if convulsed by the waters of a mighty deluge.

It has succeeded in estranging the North from the South, and in the election of a President whose administration will be infamous through all time for its subversion of popular rights; it has succeeded in the overthrow of that Constitution and Union which it has stigmatized as "a league with death and a covenant with hell;" and its triumph can be seen in the ravages of this melancholy war, in the bloody battle-fields that mark the dividing line between the North and the South, in the thousands of homes which have been made desolate throughout the country, and in the wretched, miserable attempt which is now being made by an incompetent, imbecile Administration to fasten a military despotism upon the country. It has been the faction of dissension and destruction, the party of discord and disunion; and yet its principles have been adopted in the White House, and its policy has entered largely into the management of this war. The so-called national Administration, almost from the beginning, showed a predilection for Abolitionism, and it now no

2*

longer represents the great majority of the people in its management of national affairs.

We say only what is patent when we assert that the President has violated again and again his oath of office, and that the evidence of this is to be found in the efforts of Congress to indemnify him against the consequences of his unwarrantable and unconstitutional acts.

It will hardly be denied that the President has not only acted in utter defiance of his official obligations, but that his course has been in direct antagonism with the feelings of the great conservative majority of the North. He has stamped himself for all coming time as *the* Abolition President, as the man who, misled by the designing councils of Northern disunionists, falsified his pledges to the people, and abandoning the only moderate, conservative policy which could save the country, flung himself into the hands of its enemies, and rendered useless the expenditure of the vast amount of blood and of treasure which had been poured out for the *supposed* salvation of the Republic.

Let us see if we can find any justification for his course in the sincerity of the party to whose principles and policy he yielded such a willing acquiescence. What is that party? It is known by the singularly expressive and truthful title of "ABOLITION," and its leaders are notorious for their efforts to bring the supreme law of the land into disrepute, and to overthrow a Union established by States, the majority of which were slaveholding. After more than three quarters of a century of unexampled prosperity, and the enjoyment of popular liberty to a degree that was never before realized in this world, these men have discovered that the whole system was wrong, and that the integrity of the Republic must be set aside for the furtherance of an impracticable theory. By the most persistent endeavors they have enlisted an influential portion of the press in their cause, impregnating the very literature of the North with their disorganizing influences; and yet it seems almost incredible that so far as the practical working of this principle is regarded, we can hardly, with the single exception of John Brown and his hair-brained associates, find a case of self-sacrifice among them.

Here we have been at war with the South for nearly two years, and yet no part has been taken, nor is it likely that any part will be taken, by Wendell. Phillips, Lloyd Garrison, Wilson, and Sumner, of Massachusetts, Hale, of New Hampshire, and other leading Abolitionists, in a war which is now professedly waged for the emancipation of the negro. Nay, we venture to say that the real simon-pure Abolitionists do not bear the proportion of one to every hundred in the Union army. They have not even succeeded in organizing an anti-slavery force in the whole North of two thousand. While others have been importuning for months for the ranks of colonel and brigadier-general, not one of them has ever applied for such a position, although doubtless our Abolition President would most willingly have granted their applications. True, they can point to such men as Fremont and Jim Lane; but where are the Sumners, and Giddings, and Gerrit Smiths, and Wades, and Lovejoys, and Beechers, and Cheevers, not to speak of Fred Douglass himself, the very personification and embodiment of Abolitionism?

Do we not know that Wilson organized a regiment which he never took into the field? and that both Fremont and Jim Lane have proved the most lamentable failures in the military line that ever afflicted the War Department of any country? Beecher, during the Kansas troubles, was content to call upon the people to contribute for Sharp's rifles, but he never used one. And since the fighting has commenced, we have not even heard that any regiment was called after the well-known authoress of "Uncle Tom's Cabin."

But this is not all; for we have been looking in vain for any movement on the part of the Abolitionists toward collecting money for the families of the brave fellows who have perished in a war which was brought upon the country by their wretched and ruinous policy. While they call upon others to sacrifice themselves, they refuse even to extend the hand of charity to the poor victims of their fiendish machinations to undermine the foundations of the Republic and the principles of self-government.

Never was a greater curse inflicted upon a country than that of a faction which, like the Abolitionists here and the

Orangemen in Ireland, seeks in the ascendancy of its sectional, disorganizing, and anarchical policy and measures the destruction of national unity.

The mistake of our so-called national Administration was in not making war upon this party instead of upon the South; for it is in it that our national troubles found their origin, as it is in the Abolition policy of the Administration that the leaders of the South find their justification and their strength. So long, therefore, as this party continues dominant in the North—so long as its principles find expression through the policy and acts of the Administration—no opportunity should be lost in denouncing through the press and through the assemblies of the people its insidious designs, and in warning the Administration against a compliance with its demands. If we want to get back the South, let us put down Abolitionism in the North; for so long as its councils prevail in the Cabinet, and direct the management of the war, so long will we fail in our efforts to restore peace and union to our distracted country.

WHAT IS A LOYAL LEAGUER?

(*From the* METROPOLITAN RECORD, *April* 11, 1863.)

A MAN whose patriotism is measured by his official position under the Government, or by the amounts of money received for Government contracts.

A man who desires that every one else should go to the war, but who is unwilling to risk his own precious body within reach of either cannon or rifle ball.

A man who insists that we should support the President as much when he is wrong as when he is right, and who asserts that the Emancipation Proclamation is a capital war measure.

The man who regards the Conscription Bill as the *ne plus ultra* of Congressional legislation, but who would rather pay three hundred dollars any time than shoulder a musket.

The man who, to subdue the South and hold it in military subjection, would burden the laboring classes of the North with a system of taxation even more oppressive than that of any European country.

The man who scoffs at such a thing as freedom of discussion when employed against the policy of the Administration, and who would hang every citizen that was in favor of peace.

The tax collector, the Custom House official, the Post-Office clerk, *et hoc genus omne*, who sustain the Administration because it sustains them.

The man who contends that the conservative majority are in the wrong, and the radical minority are in the right.

The man who is callous-hearted with regard to the desolation brought upon thousands of Northern homes by this cruel, unnecessary, fratricidal, and Abolition war.

The man who disregards the lessons of the past and the hopes of the future; upon whose ear the warnings of the great statesmen of the country have fallen unheeded, and who cares not how soon the Republic may be converted into a despotism.

The man who would subvert the liberties of white men or the emancipation of a race who are unfit for any other state than that of dependence.

This is a tolerably accurate sketch of the Loyal Leaguer. He is naturally such a character as constitutes the ready and willing tool of tyranny. He is acquiescent in everything which the powers that be may deem necessary toward the suppression of popular freedom. He may have taken an oath to support the Constitution, but he has not a word to say in reprobation of the usurpation of its most solemn obligations. He believes that all those rights which make the Union precious and valuable in the eyes of freemen should be held in abeyance till the Administration can wreak its wicked will in the furtherance of its Abolition and fanatical designs. What cares he for the Union as it was? What cares he for the principles of the great Revolution? He is a Government contractor, making his thousands a year by the prolongation of this war. He assumes the name of "loyal," because it agrees with his instincts, for loyalty to him has a pleasant sound. It is not allegiance to the Constitution about which he talks, but an unquestioning, slavish obedience to the behests of the Administration. He is perhaps a candidate for official promotion, and would not venture to criticise the official acts of the authorities. He is nominally an American citizen; but as for the assertion of his rights in the face of despotic power, he would not dream of such *disloyalty. He can see no difference between the Government and the Administration*, and would put down free speech with the strong arm of force; and, with the aid of Provost Marshals and the terrors of Government bastiles, would stamp out the very life and soul of American citizenship.

He has either the feelings of a despot or the cringing servility of a slave. Ask him to do his share of the fighting, and he seeks immediate refuge in the three-hundred-dollar clause of the Conscription Act. Tell him that this is a war of Emancipation and Confiscation—a war for the black man and not for the white—and he calls you a traitor. Tell him that those only are traitors who have violated the Constitution, who have broken their oath of office, and who seek refuge in a worthless indemnity bill, the very evidence of their criminality; tell him this, and he will doom you, if he have the power, to some one of those forts which were built for the protection of the country, and not for the suppression of the liberties of the citizen.

He is an Abolitionist in the true sense of the word, for he would not only abolish Slavery, but he would abolish State sovereignty, and every right guaranteed by the supreme law of the land.

We know there are men who have joined this League to whom this analysis of the character of its members will not apply, and who have been led into it from a sincere belief in its integrity of purpose; but we perceive that many have already withdrawn, having discovered its true object and designs. In fact, it has already broken up into factions, as it was found that such men and the Abolitionists could not coalesce. This is a consummation such as every good citizen should desire, and we trust that hereafter they will not be deceived by any societies that put forth as their motto, "Unconditional Loyalty to the Administration." The phrase has an unpleasant sound in the ears of a freeman, for here allegiance is due to the people by their public servants: outside of the people and the Constitution there should be no allegiance, so far as American citizenship is concerned.

GRAND PATRIOTIC DEMONSTRATION.

THE LOYAL LEAGUE OF SPOUTERS AND MUTUAL PUFFERS IN COUNCIL.

MAGNIFICENT DISPLAY OF BANNERS, BANDS, AND BATHOS.

THE VIGOROUS PROSECUTION OF THE WAR UNANIMOUSLY DEMANDED.

EXPLOSION OF A TERRIFIC BOMB-SHELL IN THE MEETING, AND UNIVERSAL SKEDADDLE OF THE PATRIOTS.

AN ANACONDA FOR THE SOUTH AND BOA-CONTRACTORS FOR THE NORTH.

[REPORTED EXCLUSIVELY FOR THE RECORD.]

(*From the* METROPOLITAN RECORD, *April* 4, 1863.)

PEDDLERS' HALL, Bunkum Square, was crowded a few weeks ago by one of the most enthusiastic gatherings which it has ever been our lot to behold.

Every man was furnished with an exact portrait of John Brown, *the first invader of the South*, while in the secret recesses of his portemonnaie lay concealed, carefully folded, a representation of the immortal Abe, printed in the highest style of art on the front of a greenback.

It is needless to say that they were all members of the Loyal League of Spouters, and strenuous upholders of the Mutual Puffing Society. Each one of these was in favor of the prolongation of the war until every slave in the South was set free and permitted to enjoy that highest privilege possessed by their colored brethren in the North, of doing nothing and of living upon something. They were also strenuous and uncompromising advocates of the right of the Government to send every poor white man to the war and to exempt every rich man therefrom on the payment of three hundred dollars. These praiseworthy objects of the Loyal League of Spouters and members of the Mutual Puffing Society ought to be sufficient to recommend them to the esteem and respect of their fellow-citizens. But there is one other feature of the organization which reflects no less creditably on its founders and its members. It is the wonderful self-abnegation which they exhibit in leaving the honors of the battle-field to be reaped by others. While they are satisfied to do the talking, the self-sacrifice which they display in allowing others to reap the laurels of military fame is beyond all praise. The Loyal League of Union Spouters are, as their name indicates, in favor of the Union to a man, and are determined to save the Republic by the most scathing and withering philippics against Jeff Davis and his rebel associates. As long as there is a greenback to be spent for contracts; as long as there is a white man to fight for the negro; as long as there is a Constitution to be ignored by the powers that be, so long will they continue their patriotic exertions.

Each man of them, at the time of his initiation into the League, took no less than ninety-nine oaths to support the President and to put down the South, and some of the leading members are earnestly engaged in sustaining the Government by their official connection with the Post-Office, the Custom-House, and other Government departments. They have been accused by their enemies of too strong a desire to remain at home; but are their accusers so blind as not to see that *somebody* must remain at home? And do they not recognize the beauty of that peculiar policy which forces all those to fight who are opposed to the war, leaving behind the men who are in favor of its vigorous prosecution to assist in collecting taxes and in electing men to office who are bound to sustain the Government despite the Constitution. What dolts, then, must the people be not to see the benefits to be derived from such a truly patriotic body as the newly-organized Loyal League of Spouters and Mutual Puffing Society.

If the readers of the RECORD are not fully acquainted

with the laudable object of those noble-minded and disinterested men, then they know not the meaning of true patriotism.

The meeting was one of the most enthusiastic ever assembled within the aqueous boundaries of our island city; and the massive walls of Peddlers' Hall resounded again and again to the plaudits of the multitude, as some crushing sentence was hurled at the Southern Confederacy, threatening to knock both it and its leaders into the middle of next week, or some "undiscovered bourne whence no traveler returns."—*Shakspeare.*

The stage was crowded with the orators of the occasion, conspicuous among whom we observed the brilliant lights of the American bar, Counselor Van Gabble and Counselor O'Puff, who were accompanied by Major-General Fleece, Honorable John Ketch, and several distinguished members of the learned professions. In front of the stage were displayed a large number of transparencies, bearing patriotic devices and inscriptions, among which the following were particularly deserving of notice:

"No compromise with Traitors."

"Conciliation is a Humbug!"

"We must sustain the President!"

"The Constitution be blowed!"

"The Three Hundred Dollar Conscription Bill forever!"

One of the branch societies of the Loyal League of Spouters exhibited a new and ingenious device on the American flag, which attracted the admiring gaze of the spectators. Instead of the square blue field on which we see emblazoned the Stars of the Union, was painted a perfect *fac simile* of a United States treasury note; while on another flag, borne by the standard-bearer of a similar society, the Goddess of Liberty was represented in a stooping posture, with the last illustrious successor of Washington perched upon her back.

There was one transparency on which was represented

a full-length portrait of a negro, with the following words inscribed beneath:

"Am I not a man and a bother?"

It will be observed that the *r* in the last word of the inscription is omitted; but this is accounted for by the fact that the sentence was painted by a designing sesesh, who had neither the fear of the President nor martial law before his eyes, and its retention was owing to the other fact, that the early education of the secretary of the society had been sadly selected, and his fellow-members had forgotten to furnish him with a copy of Webster's School Dictionary. This, however, was not the only bad *spell* with which he was occasionally afflicted; for, unlike the majority of creditors in these hard times, he was often observed to be in a state of *liquidation.*

A full band, expressly engaged for the occasion, discoursed most eloquent music, and informed the audience in melodious strains that John Brown's peripatetic soul had not yet completed its extraordinary march, and that his body as yet was in no hurry to effect a *union* with it.

We should have stated that the band was a brass one, a material which, we might say, was almost as abundant in the meeting as the greenbacks. But we will not detain our readers any longer from the intellectual treat in store for them, and shall proceed at once, therefore, to lay before them the "feast of reason and the flow of soul."

Never before had we such an opportunity of realizing the amount of *spirit* there is in the New York bar; but we shall not anticipate the *treat.*

The meeting was called to order by Hopeful Dryenuf, who expressed himself highly delighted with the scene before him, and who informed the audience that he had now no doubt whatever of the suppression of the rebellion when he witnessed the grand outpouring of men who were determined to support the Government under any and every circumstance. It was a hopeful sign of the times to behold such an enthusiastic demonstration, and to know that the respectable portion of his fellow-citizens whom he had now the pleasure of addressing was in favor of sustaining the Administration, and of setting aside the Constitution whenever it conflicted with the policy of that Administration.

A Voice: The Constitution be blowed. (Enthusiastic cheers.)

Mr. Dryenuf, resuming: That's a patriotic sentiment, and as long as we can find men willing to sacrifice *everything* for the Union, there is no danger of the—

Another Voice: The Administration.

Mr. Dryenuf: Yes, sir, the Administration, I say the Administration, and when I say the Administration I mean the Administration. [Here Counselor Van Gabble whispered something in the ear of the speaker.] It has just been suggested to me by a distinguished member of the New York bar that there are traitors in this assembly—that there is a secesh among us.

Loud cries of "Put him out," "Put him out."

Here the voice of the secesh was heard exclaiming in thunder tones that he was not in the least *put out*.

[Great excitement, uproar, and confusion, which was only calmed by two or three enthusiastic committeemen seizing the greenback banner, and waving it in utter defiance of the rebellious secesh.]

Peace having been restored, the Honorable Mr. Dryenuf expressed the supreme felicity he had in introducing Mr. Musing, of the *Daily Abolition Stick*, whose verses to a barn-yard fowl are considered by critics to be superior to that celebrated ode on an expiring frog immortalized in the doings of the Pickwick Club.

After stating that he was rejoiced to see so many Loyal Leaguers and mutual puffers present, he pleasantly and facetiously informed them that as brevity was the soul of wit, he would not afflict them with a long speech, preferring to leave that task to others who were more capable. He was, he informed them, unaccustomed to public speaking, and he hoped, therefore, that they would not expect a speech from him. He was no orator like some of those he saw around him.

A Voice: Louder.

Here Counselor Van Gabble whispered a few words in the ear of the poic.

Mr. Musing: It has been suggested to me by a member of the bar, who is distinguished—

A Voice: Extinguished, you mean. (Vociferous cries from all sides of Peddlers' Hall of "Put that man out! he's a traitor." More uproar, which was only calmed by the renewed waving of the greenback banner.)

Mr. Musing, resuming: I said distinguished.

Two or three voices: You said that before.

Mr. Musing: Yes, and I'll say it again. I repeat, a distinguished member of the bar has just suggested that the Government must be sustained at every sacrifice. But, gentlemen, as I informed you before, I am not a public speaker. I can handle the pen with more dexterity than the tongue, and you know the pen is mightier than the sword. (Great applause from the speakers and invited guests on the stage.) Yes, gentlemen, I say the pen is mightier than the sword. (Renewed enthusiastic demonstrations from the stage.)

A Voice: That's the reason, I suppose, none of you fellows take the sword. (Terrific demonstrations were here made against the invisible voice, and one gallant individual on the stage informed the Loyal Leaguers and Mutual Puffers that if the owner of that voice could be found, he should be hung without judge or jury, or the benefit of habeas corpus.)

Mr. Musing, when peace was restored, again told the audience that he was unaccustomed to public speaking, and would have continued to enlighten them on the same subject, were it not for the impatience of the next speaker on the programme, who pulled him so violently by the coat-tails as to seriously endanger the poic's perpendicular. After informing his audience, therefore, that his feelings were too deep for utterance, and that under the circumstances he felt unable to address them at further length, he took his seat, and was more vehemently applauded for this act than at any time during his remarks.

His place was taken by the gentleman who had made such dangerous demonstrations on his coat-tails as to cause serious fears in the mind of the speaker that his caudal extremity would be dislocated. In consequence of this gentleman's extreme modesty, we have concluded, out of respect to his feelings, not to publish his name, and, for the same cogent reason, we regret to say we are obliged to omit his speech. However, it may be interesting to know that this gentleman informed an inquisitive Irishman that the people of this country were descended from England, but that there were some Germans who fought "mit Sigel." We may say that a friend of this gentleman furnished us with the manuscript of his speech, but our limited space obliges us, however, reluctantly to forego the gratification of presenting it in full to our readers.

At this part of the proceedings a distinguished Government official arrived, and informed the President that the Administration was about to give out more contracts, and that the patriotic gentlemen to whom those contracts were awarded would be paid without delay. That they might not be kept waiting, it had been concluded by the Administration to retain the pay of the soldiers for this laudable purpose. He further informed the President that the Government currency mills were kept in operation day and night, so that there should be no lack of the great and glorious greenbacks. The Government, he further said, had withheld the pay from the soldiers lest, out of disgust for the abolition proclamation, they should incontinently skedaddle. The President said nothing, but, shutting his sinister eye, gave a wink that expressed volumes.

One of the Vice-Presidents was heard to say in an under tone that they would stand by the President as long as he had a greenback in the Treasury.

This pleasant little interlude having terminated, the Honorable Counselor O'Puff, who was said to be a sort of cousin-german in the political line to his professional associate, Honorable Counselor Van Gabble, and who also never forgets to commend himself to the consideration of his audience by humorously informing them that he is a native of the Sixth Ward, and that he can trace his descent from Celtic ancestors, took the floor.

A Voice: Yes, begorra, and a mighty great descent, too.

Counselor Van Gabble here came over and whispered something in the legal ear of his brother.

Counselor O'Puff: It has been suggested to me by my learned friend that I should take no notice of these vulgar interruptions; but I must say I will not allow my name to be trifled with, since the Mutual Puffers have done me the honor to use it as the title of their society.

A Voice: Bah! what's in a name?

(Loud cries of "Put him out," "Hoist him," "Hang him," etc.)

Counselor O'Puff, deprecatingly, with his right hand waving in magnificent style, and his left feeling about the region of his stomach for his heart, said: Allow me to answer that man. I tell you, sir, there's a great deal in a name, and I, sir, am a living exemplification of that fact. I have been accused of making too much of my name, and some base enemies of mine have insisted that I am too fond of talking about it; but I have nothing for them but the language of contempt and of scorn. I know there is some doubt as to the place of my nativity; but, sir, unlike most other men, I have had two birthplaces, for I have had the good fortune to be a native of Ireland and America at the same time. But, gentlemen, *as I can not get rid of my name*, I must tell you that, under the circumstances, I think it is a very good one; and, like Mrs. Micawber, I shall never—no, never—desert the family of the O'Puffs. (Immense cheering.) The South, gentlemen of the Loyal League and Puffing Society, has called us Yankees; but let me say that I am deadly opposed to the manufacture of wooden hams and nutmegs; for, however much they may be relished by others, I must say that they don't suit my taste. (This joke of the facetious and witty speaker set the audience in a roar, and affected the President so much as to bring tears to his eyes. An obstreperous son of Connecticut who was present took exception to the joke, and insisted that such reflections were highly invidious, and reflected injuriously on two of the most essential articles of commerce from his native State.) The honorable counselor proceeded, and assured the gentleman that he was a friend of Connecticut; that he was an ardent admirer of P. T. Barnum; that if that State had done nothing else than to give to the world those wonderful specimens of the human race, General Tom Thumb and his Liliputian bride, it had laid the world under a debt of gratitude which it could never repay. (This mollified the native of the Nutmeg State; and having stated that the apology was satisfactory, and that there would be no occasion for either coffee or pistols, he resumed his seat and his temper at the same time.)

Mr. O'Puff resumed by informing the audience that he was a bachelor himself, and, to use the language of that great creation of Dickens, Sairy Gamp, "he was not likely." Yet, he must say that no man had a greater regard for the fair sex than he; but his single-blessedness was owing to the difficulty he had in making a choice, for invidious distinctions were a thing that he despised. He had never yet responded to a toast upon "woman," that he had not felt in his heart of hearts that the subject was too much for him. This, however, he must say was a failing of the O'Puff family, for woman was a subject to which he could never do justice. He regretted greatly that he could not agree with the women of the South, and it was a sad thing for him to reflect that they were not in favor of union—to a man. He would say, however, that if the Northern women came out a little stronger in favor of the Administration, that there would be more Northern men in the field.

A Voice: Why ain't you in the field?

Because, said Mr. O'Puff—

(Great confusion. Cries of, "Toss him out! traitor! secesh!")

Mr. O'Puff resuming: Gentlemen, let me answer that man. (Loud cries of, "Go in, O'Puff! Give it to him!") That individual wants to know why I am not in the field. Let me tell him that the reason I am not in the field is because I am here. ("Hurra, hurra, hurra! O'Puff forever.")

Having effectually squelched this double-dyed traitor, the learned gentleman resumed his seat amid vociferous cheers, in the midst of which his cousin-german, Counselor Van Gabble, came over and shook him most affectionately by the hand. Whereupon the cheers broke out afresh, and one gentleman on the stage clapped his hands so energetically as to destroy a new pair of kid gloves which he had that morning bought on credit. Another individual was so overcome by his enthusiasm that he pounded a new table, which the proprietor of Peddlers' Hall had purchased the day before, in such a violent manner as to arouse the fears of the owner in regard to its safety. The aforesaid proprietor mildly informed him that that very necessary article of domestic furniture had cost him the sum of five dollars, and he further informed him that five dollars were not to be had every day. After furnishing this interesting piece of intelligence, he retired with the most amiable expression of countenance.

Mr. Mudley Hill followed the last-named speaker, and succeeded in impressing upon his audience that he was in favor of a vigorous prosecution of the war. Our reporter would have taken full notes of his remarks were it not for the annoyance to which he was subjected by two small boys in his vicinity, one of whom would insist in sticking pins into the other, under the threat that he would punch him in the head if he would not submit to this innocent and pleasant little means of torture. A red-nosed gentleman sitting near became seriously perturbed the moment he heard the sound of *punch*, and mentally resolved that as soon as the meeting was over he would pay the first liquor-dealer he met on his way home to give him a *punch* in the mouth.

According to the programme, as prepared by a committee of contractors, resolutions of a most patriotic character were read by a large gentleman with a weak voice, who was frequently interrupted by demands of the most unreasonable nature. He was invited to "speak louder," to "raise his voice," to "go it stronger," and to "talk up," all of which invitations, for reasons sufficient to himself, he was obliged to decline. However, our indefatigable corps of reporters succeeded in getting a copy from the gentleman on condition that they would print his name; but we are exceedingly mortified at not being able to perform our part of the contract, in consequence of the treacherous memory of the aforesaid corps of reporters. But here are the resolutions, and they will speak for themselves:

Whereas, This war has been waged for two years without any prospect of conquering the South; and

Whereas, Armies numbering in the aggregate fifteen hundred thousand men, and money to the amount of nearly fifteen hundred millions of dollars have been freely given by the people; and

Whereas, What the people did before, they will most probably do again; and

Whereas, It is essential to the policy of the Administration that the Constitution should not be allowed to hamper its movements, and that the liberty of the citizen should be held in abeyance; and

Whereas, The war is a very profitable speculation to contractors and officeholders generally; and

Whereas, The doctrine of State Rights is an exploded humbug, and Constitutional rights tolerably good things for the age of the Revolution, but particularly inappropriate to the present times; and

Whereas, George Washington, Thomas Jefferson, and James Madison were all very well for *their* time but not for *our* time; and

Whereas, We find this war pays splendidly, and is likely to pay as long as it lasts; and

Whereas, A minority President should not regard the will of the majority when it conflicts with administrative patriotism; and

Whereas, We have no objection to pay any amount of taxes so long as it comes out of the pockets of the laboring classes; and

Whereas, There is a certain class of people in our midst who are opposed to the war for the foolish reason that it can not restore the Union; and

Whereas, We are bound to support the Administration through thick and thin, against the Constitution, against State Rights, against habeas corpus, against the liberty of the press, against the conservative majority of the people, and against popular freedom; therefore,

Resolved, That this war be continued as long as there is a dollar to be made by contractors and railroad corporations, which do the carrying business of the West formerly done on the Mississippi, and that all who are opposed to its vigorous prosecution are traitors, who should be hung on the first lamp-post.

Resolved, That the conduct of so-called citizens of these United States, in talking of such nonsense as fraternity of feeling with the South, brotherly love, or any such stuff as that, should be judged guilty of disloyalty and high treason, and be forthwith sent to Fort Lafayette, or any of the numerous bastiles throughout the country.

Resolved, That we, the people of New York, now assembled in Peddlers' Hall, hereby figuratively and metaphorically pledge our fortunes, and also pledge so much as we have left of our influence and honor, to support the Administration in its vigorous and determined efforts to do *something*, and especially in its vigorous prosecution of the war and Northern citizens.

Resolved, That every man in the army and navy of the United States must be re-sworn to the support of the Constitution if he should grumble about not receiving his pay.

Resolved, That as the great Lord Castlereagh, so well known to Irishmen, thanked Heaven that he had a country to sell, so we also return thanks that we have a Constitution to violate.

Resolved, That every citizen owes allegiance to Abraham Lincoln, President of the United States; and he who denies his authority to do what he pleases, should suffer the penalty due to his crime.

Resolved, That the man whose term of service is about to expire should be compelled to remain until they receive their pay.

Resolved, That this meeting, having a firm reliance on the President and his Secretary of War, hereby resolves itself into a Loyal League of Spouters and Mutual Puffing Society, pledged to an indefinite prolongation of the war, and to the prosecution of all who insist that this Union can be preserved by any other means than the sword and the unlimited issue of greenbacks.

These resolutions were received with the most unbounded applause and unanimously adopted, with the exception of four or five obstreperous individuals who would persist, like the President of the United States, in opposing the will of the majority. The vocal band of the Loyal League of Spouters and Mutual Puffing Society here came forward to the front of the stage, and, silence having been restored, sang the following beautiful and highly expressive song:

SONG OF THE LOYAL LEAGUERS.

AIR—"*The Wedding of Ballyporeen.*"

What nonsense to prate about Freedom and Right;
He has freedom enough who has freedom to fight;
So, shoulder your muskets and muzzle your clack,
And a war-charger make of each old party hack.
Then, hurrah for strong, vigorous measures!
Hurrah for strong, vigorous measures!
Hurrah for strong, vigorous measures!
Some good, healthy hanging for me!

Down, down with the traitors who clamor for peace;
Make war upon them and our troubles will cease;
Or give them an office and peace they'll forego,
For no placemen are peacemen, I'd have you to know;
For they go for strong, vigorous measures!
They go for strong, vigorous measures!
They go for strong, vigorous measures!
No peacemen or traitors are they.

Our Government's strong and our Government's wise,
And, mark me! 'twill soon take the world by surprise;
For I've telegrams got, and this way they run:
"Look out! something somewhere will shortly be done!"
Then, hurrah for strong, vigorous measures!
Hurrah for strong, vigorous measures!
Hurrah for strong, vigorous measures!
Some healthy blood-letting for me!

At the chorus the whole meeting joined in, and it was mutually resolved that the author of the song should get a place in the Custom-House. When the feelings which had been aroused by this truly patriotic effusion of the muse were calmed, the Honorable Counselor Van Gabble arose and confronted the audience. He said he was a Loyal Leaguer, for loyalty to him had a pleasant sound ever since that happy and festive evening when he tripped on the light fantastic toe with the present incumbent of the English throne.

In every sense of the word, then, he was a loyal man. (Cries of "Louder!") Mr. Van Gabble: If I am *allowed* to proceed, my voice will get louder. I know the full compass of my voice, and I know it will reach every part and corner of this building. But before I proceed further, let me inform you that I am a friend of General Scott, and have dined at the same club-table with him, and if you should have any doubts of this I will send his next letter to me for publication in the *Daily Abolition Stick*. I approve of everything my friend Mr. O'Puff has uttered, and as you have doubtless observed, I have made suggestions to the different speakers in the course of their remarks—suggestions of a highly patriotic and loyal nature. (Tremendous cheering.) I want you to stand by the President in everything; for, although he has issued his Emancipation Proclamation, take my word for it, he is not an abolitionist. In the language of the race-course, let me inform you that he is a cross of Kentucky upon Illinois. (Applause.) The only question in my judgment worth considering is, how are we to carry on the war? and this is a question of serious moment, for this is a war not only against the South, but against the Constitution. (Cheers, and cries of "That's it.") I told you some months ago that I was in favor of liberty of speech—and now I am in favor of liberty of speech for all who support the Administration. I am in favor of a vigorous prosecution of the war; I am in favor of capturing Vicksburg, and if it don't stay captured, I am in favor of capturing it till it does. I know that the Administration has published dispatches driving them out of that fortification, but they wouldn't stay out, and I trust that they will be dispatched at last.

I am down on peace, and opposed to everybody that is in favor of peace.

A *Voice*: How about the "Wayward Sisters?" (Great laughter.)

Let me answer that man. I have thought better of that, and I am determined that the Sisters shall do a little more fighting. I was opposed to the last two proclamations of the President; but as he issued them before I had a chance to oppose them, I must say that I am decidedly in favor of them now. I can pick out any number of flaws in the Conscription Law, but I am in favor of every line of it. I don't object to the suspension of the writ of habeas corpus; and although it was not suspended in the war of the Revolution nor in the war of 1812, yet both those wars were successful. So far as the President's proclamation is concerned, I see nothing wrong in it. It is a very good proclamation, and every way worthy of the author of that sublime saying, "It is easier to do nothing than it is to do something."

Here the President whispered something in the speaker's ear.

Mr. Van Gabble: It has been suggested to me by our worthy President that such papers as the METROPOLITAN RECORD, or any other journal that is in favor of such treason as the liberty of speech, should be immediately suppressed, and its editor sent to Fort Lafayette. (Great applause, and cries of, "Give it to him, Van Gabble." "Hit him again.") It is gratifying to know that Russia is favorable to us. (Cheers.) Gentlemen, we can not be too thankful to that nation. Let us trust that the Emperor will put down the Poles as we are trying to do with the South, and that when he gets them down he'll keep them down. In this respect there is a common bond of sympathy between us, for if he is opposed to the liberty of the people, so are we. (Cheers.) We are getting nearer to his style of government every day, and it will not be the fault of our worthy President and his statesmanlike cabinet if we do not succeed in finally establishing among ourselves the principles of absolutism. Now, gentlemen, I have been accused of being on every side of the question, but let me tell you that it is only by getting on every side of it that you can tell exactly how it looks. I have now taken my last stand *until the next time*, and I shall never disgrace the great name I have inherited from my worthy paternal progenitor. I shall now conclude, gentlemen, and should I receive any more letters, you may depend upon their publication in the *Daily Abolition Stick*. The learned gentleman here took his seat amid the most uproarious enthusiasm.

At this stage of the proceedings considerable commotion was visible on the stage in consequence of the appearance of a committee of gentlemen in favor of a vigorous prosecution of the war. The Chairman desired to address a few words to the meeting, which permission was generously granted by the President. He then came forward and spoke as follows:

Gentlemen of the Loyal League of Spouters and Mutual Puffing Society—In connection with the gentlemen who have accompanied me, I have been deputed by a number of the loyal citizens of this metropolis to make a proposition to this meeting which, I have no doubt, will prove highly acceptable. (Cries of, "Hear him—hear him!")

Gentlemen, this is a large meeting; there must at least be three thousand persons present.

A Voice: More than that.

Well, gentlemen, are you all in favor of a vigorous prosecution of the war? (Loud cries of, "We are—we are.") Will you go for the President right or wrong? (Loud cries of, "We will—we will.") That, gentlemen, is what I call true patriotism. (Cheers.) Now, then, gentlemen, I am commissioned to say, that as you are in favor of a vigorous prosecution of the war, and of sustaining the President right or wrong, the patriotic gentlemen by whom we are commissioned have pledged themselves to provide every man of you with a uniform and a musket, and to pay your expenses all the way down to the army of the Potomac.

Great consternation was caused by this announcement among the audience, in the midst of which a large portion of it, finding the place inconveniently warm, succeeded in getting into the fresh air with extraordinary rapidity. Mr. Van Gabble, Mr. O'Puff, Mr. Mudley Hill, and several other prominent supporters of the Government, with astonishing unanimity sprang to their feet and moved for an immediate adjournment, which the President put to the meeting without further delay; and having taken the ayes, concluded, without regard to the nays, that the meeting was adjourned.

Thus ended the great mass meeting at Peddlers' Hall, Bunkum Square; and thus may all who are in favor of a vigorous prosecution of the war escape the designs of deep-dyed traitors, who imagine that a man can not sustain the Administration as well in the Post-Office or Custom-House as on the field of battle. None but a secesh can understand that if an anaconda is necessary to squeeze the life out of the South, it is not equally necessary that the life of the North should be squeezed out by BOA-CONTRACTORS.

[NOTE BY REPORTER.—It is only a tribute to true merit and patriotism to state that the conduct of Counselors O'Puff and Van Gabble is beyond all praise, particularly when it is known that to serve the Administration they have not hesitated to forego all prospects of political promotion hereafter.]

SOME PLAIN TALK.

(*From the* METROPOLITAN RECORD *of April* 18, 1863.)

IT is now two years since the war commenced, and we are to-day further than ever from the attainment of the object which the Administration is said to have in view—the restoration of the Union. Armies, numbering in the aggregate fourteen or fifteen hundred thousand men, and money to the amount of about fifteen hundred millions of dollars, have been placed at the disposal of the President; and yet, with all our boasted superiority in population and material resources, we have less chance to-day of reducing the South to submission than we had when the first gun was fired at Fort Sumter.

We ask any candid man if this is not a fair, though brief statement of the relative positions occupied at present by the North and the South? Still we are told, "this war must go on; we are in for it now, and we can not, if we would, make peace short of national disgrace and humiliation." "What!" says an enthusiastic Loyal Leaguer, "shall we submit to Jeff Davis? Shall we sue to the rebel South for peace? No, sir; this war must go on, even if we were to shed the last drop of our blood and spend our last dollar." Now, let us remark that the man who talks in this inflated strain is the very last to think of shedding the first drop of his own blood, or to spend the first dollar of his own money, unless, indeed, he be compelled to do so by the unlucky chances of the conscription lottery. In fact, we are inclined to think that if he could save the expense through the favoritism of the War Department, he would be most happy to place himself upon the list of exempts.

So much, then, for the sincerity of those who clamor for the continuance of this melancholy, this fratricidal war—a war, not for the restoration of the country, but for the continued power and domination of a faction. But how is it with the great body of the people? Are they still in favor of a perpetuation of a conflict which threatens the establishment of a permanent military despotism, and which is already pressing with terrible weight upon the laboring classes of the country? We sincerely believe that they are not, and that if they were presented with the opportunity of giving their decision, it would be in favor of an armistice with a view to a peaceful settlement of the armed controversy now waging between the two sections. We believe, moreover, that they have lost all confidence in the Administration, and that the last hope of a restoration of the Union through war has departed from the great popular heart.

It is true that the so-called leaders of the people are opposed to the suspension of hostilities; but let us ask, do they really speak for the people? Have they been commissioned as their mouthpieces to give expression to such views? For our own part we must say, that they do not express the feelings of the great majority of the Northern masses in regard to the prolongation of the war. Many of them have not the manliness nor the courage to say what they really believe, that the longer continuance of this war will render the restoration of the Union hereafter an impossibility, This is no time for mincing the matter. We have had enough of temporizing and political hypocrisy, and it is full time to look the question squarely in the face without flinching, no matter what the timid or nervous may say.

This is no longer war. It is slaughter; it is rapine, and the acts that have come to light lately show a vandalism that reflects the deepest disgrace on a nation which professes to be Christian. We have had enough of expediency, enough of time-serving, enough of hypocritical professions of loyalty, and we must at last deal with the hard facts of the case. In the first place, the past two years should satisfy us of two things—that the military subjugation of the South is an impossibility; and in the second, that the present disunion Administration can not restore the Union. These are the two leading facts presented by a consideration of the case; but there are some others which we propose to review before dismissing the subject for the present, and we shall submit them in the following brief, but, we trust, sufficiently comprehensive and intelligible manner.

The people of the South are at the present time more hostile to the old Union than they were two years, or even one year ago. This result has been brought about by the Abolition and sectional policy of the Administration.

The restoration of the Union by war was a departure from the well-known policy of conciliation and compromise, and was calculated to render division permanent.

The invasion of the South was the maddest project ever devised by men professing to be statesmen, inevitably leading, as it has done, to the consolidation of the Southern States into a unit for the purpose of determined and aggressive resistance.

The people of the North have lost all trust and confidence in the Administration—a fact which is attributable to its unconstitutional course and its utter incompetency.

The upopularity of an unjust, a one-sided, and oppressive Conscription Act which discriminates between the rich and the poor, in favor of the former and against the latter.

The repulse sustained at Fredericksburg, at Port Hudson, at Vicksburg, Charleston, and other places.

The mad and wicked policy of supposing that Americans could conquer Americans, or that the freemen of the South could be subdued by an Abolition faction, or would ever submit to an Administration which set at defiance all constitutional restraints, and obstinately refused to offer any terms of conciliation or compromise.

The Confiscation Act, which placed the property of our Southern fellow-citizens at the disposal of courts which had no constitutional existence, and at the mercy of such men as he who brought disgrace upon the national character and a stain upon the national flag by his inhuman course as military governor of New Orleans.

The burning of cities, the wanton destruction of private property, as in the case of Jacksonville.

The emancipation of slaves, and the overthrow of State limits.

In these facts are to be found some of the prominent causes which are daily widening the chasm between the North and the South, and which will render union, even in the far-distant future, almost an impossibility.

Now, we say, in consideration of all these facts, the feelings of the people should not be disguised. If their so-called leaders are prevented by expediency, or by political hypocrisy, from a fair and candid exposition of their views and opinions, and if the Administration should be deceived (which we think is not at all probable) by them as to the real sentiments of the masses, they may be made aware of it by the most terrific popular revolution that ever convulsed a country. Let us not be misunderstood in this matter. We deprecate anything like an armed uprising of the people so long as they are left the freedom of discussion in public meetings, and the right of deciding on public questions through the ballot-box. But have we not been made painfully aware already that even the ballot-box is not sacred from the invasion and encroachments of the faction in power? It is but a few days since the democratic voters in Indianapolis were driven from the polls by soldiers who it is said were sent there for that very purpose; while in Connecticut it is insisted that the volunteers of the Union army, whose political principles were previously subjected to a test, were employed by the

Administration in voting down a political opponent whose peace principles had rendered him obnoxious to the war party.

Well may we fear for social order in the Northern States. Well may the voice of warning be raised against a policy that, if persisted in, will, it is justly feared, bring civil war and anarchy into the North. If we would avert such a calamity, we must have peace—not a humiliating peace, but a peace between two belligerent powers, who, after having tried in vain to end the controversy by the sword, might justly resort to an armistice as a much more reasonable course of settling the question. To this we must come at last. The sword will never solve the difficulty. Let us then have peace. Surely the faction that rules at Washington has had enough of blood-letting. Surely the political cormorants have had enough of public plunder.

The prolongation of this war will inevitably lead to despotism. Which do we prefer—to let the South go, or to lose our own liberties in an attempt to force it unwillingly into a union with us; and when to keep it in such a union we would require an army of occupation in every Southern State numbering at least a million of men? For our own part we must say that we prefer liberty to Union on such terms, and if that be treason, make the most of it.

"NOBODY'S HURT."

(*From the* Metropolitan Record, *April* 18, 1863.)

Two years ago the United States were at the summit of earthly prosperity. Kingdoms gray with centuries sought its alliance; nations whose record was the history of civilization gazed with wonder on the new star that appeared in the political firmament; the oppressor looked to it with wondering dread, and the oppressed with yearning love and reverence. In every tongue it was a synonym for freedom, and its example fired the heart and nerved the arm of struggling patriots in every land.

America! the very name suggested images of smiling peace and plenty—a land flowing with milk and honey—a people prosperous and contented—honored abroad and happy at home. No citizen of Rome, in Rome's palmiest days, bore a prouder title than he who hailed from the Republic of the West. Then an American citizen meant a freeman—one who owned no lord, "saving the Lord on high," who held his rights at the option of no petty despot, who owed allegiance only to his country and fealty only to his God. From Maine to Texas, from the Atlantic to the Pacific seaboard, resounded the hum of thriving industry, for peace was within our borders, and we were at peace with the world without. Two short years ago we might have defied the world in arms; now we tremble at the thought of intervention. Two short years ago the complications in European politics were of no account to us, save when our sympathies were aroused by the gallant struggle of some oppressed nationality; now, we look to these uprisings as a providential diversion in our favor, and calculate the effect they will have on the duration and ultimate result of our war of the sections. Why is this? and why is there sorrow in our dwellings and wailing throughout the land? "*Nobody's hurt.*"

"Nobody's hurt!" Yet, on the plains and in the valleys of Virginia fell thousands upon thousands of American citizens, whose death left a gap in many a fireside circle, an aching void in many a desolate heart, who died without religious consolation or medical aid—without the soothing ministrations of friends or the loving care of kindred—amid the horrors of battle, with the sound of carnage, or the rush of charging squadrons, or the groans of wounded comrades in their ears, with the earth for a pillow and the wind for a requiem.

"Nobody's hurt!" Yet, from the waters of the Mississippi, from the harbor of Charleston, and from the waves of the ocean and the Gulf comes up a gurgling cry, heard faintly and at intervals amid the iron storm that lashes the waters into frenzy, and this cry gives the lie direct to the axiomatized untruth.

"Nobody's hurt!" Yet, every day our forces dwindle and our Army of the Dead increases; *for Death has is-*

sued a Conscription Bill, and he draws his quota chiefly from our great military centers.

"Nobody's hurt!" Yet, there is grief in wooden shanties and brown-stone mansions, in town and country, at home and abroad. Our troubles have paralyzed the manufactures of England, they have discouraged the commerce of France, they have violently changed the course of European emigration. But what of that? "Nobody's hurt!" North and South are bleeding at every pore; the life-blood of the nation is oozing out drop by drop, immense tracts are laid waste, fertile districts are depopulated, the national prestige is lost, the national wealth dissipated, the national credit destroyed, the national honor tarnished, but—*nobody's hurt.* That glorious anti-climax reassures us, "Nobody's hurt!" Hark, how the echoing chorus swells from Manassas and Fredericksburg, from Shiloh and Antietam, from Vicksburg and New Orleans, from the Potomac and the Mississippi. "NOBODY'S HURT!!"

Tell it to that miserable woman, with her helpless, starving family; tell it to those orphans thrown upon the cold charity of an unfeeling world, or to that old man trembling on the brink of the grave, or to those troops of maimed and wounded soldiers who are thrown back upon their State like so much damaged goods—tell them, if you dare, that "nobody's hurt." That woman's husband went down in the ill-fated Cumberland; those children's father fell at Edward's Ferry; that old man's sole support was trampled under the hoofs of Stuart's cavalry; that wounded soldier lost his arm where many a gallant comrade lost his life, on the banks of the bloody Rappahannock. Tell *them* "nobody's hurt."

And when you have had the moral hardihood to do that, then turn to the Administration, every member of which, from the President down to the lowest officer, has lost character and reputation, the respect of the civilized world, and the regard of their fellow-citizens; lost not only political capital, but political *life;* and tell them "nobody's hurt." It is probable they could understand the force of the saying better to-day than two short years ago. Then they were starting on their four-years' cruise, elate and sanguine; now they lie stranded on the breakers, the good ship Constitution battered on all sides, the crew fearfully diminished, the supplies gone, the reckoning lost. Now ring in their ears the mocking cry with which they started—"Nobody's hurt."

PEACE!

(*From the* METROPOLITAN RECORD, *April* 25, 1863.)

THE country is sick of this aimless, brutal slaughter, and yearns for peace. From every desolate homestead, where widowed mothers and fatherless children dwell in the destitution of uncared-for, unthought-of penury; from every battle-field in whose festering trenches lie the tens of thousands drawn from the peaceful army of labor by the *conscription of death;* from an over-taxed, despot-ridden population; from the ranks of industry, for which the Conscript Act was exclusively designed; from the prostrate commerce of our Atlantic sea-board, and the profitless agriculture of the teeming West, arises the imperative demand for peace. The people are now aware that the war can never restore the Union; that they have been cruelly deceived; that the men whom they raised to the highest official positions have abused the confidence reposed in them; that their money is squandered to swell the wealth of political harpies; that the brave men who went forth to fight *for the Union* have been sacrificed to the fell spirit of Abolitionism; and that after a two years' war we are no nearer the restoration of the Union than we were at its commencement. It is, we believe, no exaggeration to say that nearly half a million of men have been killed outright upon the battle-field, have died of their wounds, and of diseases incident to camp life, or have been flung, maimed for life, dependents on their friends or the benevolence of the public. All this they know; and they know, moreover, from the painful experience of the past, that the same incompetency, the same imbecility, the same official corruption, the same fanaticism, the same disregard of popular opinion, the same reckless expenditure of blood and money, the same heartless indifference for their bleeding country, prevails at this moment among the authorities in Washington. From those they have nothing to hope, and they must, therefore, look to themselves for the remedy. They have learned, as their first political lesson, that this is a Government of the people; that they are the source of all power, and that their officials are their servants, bound by the most solemn obligations to do their will, as contained and expressed in the Constitution and laws of the land. Knowing this, and knowing also that the Constitution has been put aside, has been set at defiance, they should rouse themselves to meet the emergency; they should assemble in mass meetings all over the country, until the popular voice, increasing in volume as the great movement goes on, should reverberate in thunder tones throughout the land, so that even official deafness should hear, and hearken to the demand for peace.

We know there are some who have grown supine and hopeless; who say that the war can not be stayed; that it will be carried on during the whole term of the present Administration.

It is true that we have become reckless in the waste of human life, that we who shrank from the very idea of civil war have come to regard it as a matter of course, that it has become, as it were, a fixed subject in our daily habits of thought, and it is also true that, if we don't take care, the new interests which have sprung up—which have increased, and which now depend upon the continuance of the war for their very existence—will render the re-establishment of peace a work of serious difficulty. But, after all, there is a bright side to the subject. The election returns which reach us week by week give unmistakable evidence in their conservative course of the change that is taking place in the public mind. Despite the efforts of Government officials, despite the intermeddling of the Administration with State elections, despite the operations and influence of shoddy and other contractors who discharge the honest workman that dares to vote as his conscience dictates, despite the threats of a General-in-Chief who tells the peace men of the North that he will crush them out with military force—despite, we say, of all this, the people are resolved that they will be heard at the Capital of the Nation, and that a war which is now carried on mainly for the benefit of political partisans and Abolitionists must soon come to an end. No matter what desperate efforts may be made through official machinery to revive the war enthusiasm which two years ago swept over the land like a plague, no matter what scheming and chicanery may be resorted to in the way of Loyal Leagues and so-called Union Meetings, the people have had enough of war, and are now thoroughly convinced that blood-letting is no panacea for the ills of the Nation.

We tell the Administration that the game of war can not be played any longer; that, like every other species of gambling, it requires capital, and that the great public credit upon which they have drawn so largely will shortly refuse to honor their drafts. The ingenious scheme of *three-months-political promissory notes* has been tried too often and has been found not to pay. In fact, the balance of interest is on the wrong side of the account. A depleted population, a bankrupted credit, an imbecile Administration, incompetent generals, a dissatisfied army, an over-taxed and discontented people—all of these form rather unreliable supports in the further prosecution of the war. We would, therefore, advise the President and his Cabinet seriously to reflect upon the circumstances in which they are placed, and to make up their mind before it is too late—*before the failure of the Conscription Act*—to take such preliminary measures as are necessary to bring about peace. There is no disguising the fact that the attempt to abolitionize the war has created a wide-spread feeling of discontent throughout the army, while Vicksburg, Port Hudson, and, lastly, the terrible disaster at Charleston, have satisfied the North that the men of the South have inherited from their revolutionary sires that unconquerable spirit, that indomitable will that knows no yielding.

Let us ask ourselves would we not fight to the last gasp against an invading army, and would not the sight of ruined homes, burning cities, and desecrated churches arouse in our breasts the same feelings which have thus far rendered, and which will continue to render, the military conquest of the South an impossibility. No man who possesses a heart can refuse his admiration to the spectacle of a gallant people engaged in a struggle for what they regard as the cause of national independence, and the right to live under that form of government which they are resolved to maintain at every sacrifice. Seven or eight millions of a population successfully contending against a section of the continent numbering at least twenty-two millions, is something of a disproportion; but then it must be remembered that they are united, and that they are fighting against an Administration which had its origin in the spirit of disunion. Let us at once admit that we can never conquer such a people, and accept the inevitable consequence which must follow from the admission—PEACE. To this it will be objected that peace is *recognition;* but that is not the view we take of it. We desire to have peace *as the only means left of developing a Union sentiment in the South.* And here let us say that the invasion of that section of our country not only overwhelmed that element, but brought about *a union of the whole South against the Union.* Any policy leading to such a result should have been rejected by the Administration. Invasion of sovereign States, even under the provocation of the attack on Fort Sumter, should never have been determined upon. The Southern leaders knew well that the appearance of an invading army upon the soil of the South would arouse a feeling of indignation that would unite their whole people against the North. What, then, it may be asked, should have been the course of the President under the circumstances? Recognizing the peculiar character of our Government, and the fact that it is the representative of aggregate Sovereignties, his course should have been that of conciliation and compromise. The idea of the dignity of the country being at stake, and having been insulted by an assault upon the national flag, is nothing more or less than nonsense, and the time that has been made about it is simply political claptrap. It was not insulted by a foreign power; but we should never forget that we have been subjected to more humiliation and disgrace by the men at Washington, whom, unfortunately in an evil hour, we intrusted with the destinies of the Republic. If we are in search of insults, let us not look for them among our own countrymen of the

South, but rather among those who were the allies and bosom friends of the Abolitionists, the British enemies of the Republic, who are now building privateers to prey upon our commerce, and who find in the fanatics who rule at the National Capital the strongest adherents of their "divide-and-ruin" policy. Insult! Who could insult freemen more than those who have prostrated our blood-bought rights? who fling scorn and contempt on the martyred heroes of the Revolution by telling us that the Constitution which they gave their lives to establish is "a leage with Death and a covenant with Hell?" Away, then, with this cant about insult, and our National honor having been trampled in the dust. If the men of the North have been beaten again and again upon Southern battle-fields, it has been done by Americans and not by a foreign power, and let it be remembered that they have been beaten, too, while *fighting under an Abolition Administration.* It is not because the men of the South are more brave than those of the North, but because of the difference in the characters of the leaders of both sections.

We know with what succcss this trick about the insult to our flag was practiced upon the too sensitive credulity of the North, leading it astray from the only wise and politic course, which was that of patience and forbearance. We now say what we have always believed from the very beginning, that if the South had been appealed to by the memories of the Revolution to sustain the Union which had been formed by Northern and Southern men, there would have been aroused such a feeling of love and devotion to it throughout the whole South as would have overborne all opposition.

But if the men at Washington have proved false to the country and to their solemn pledges, we must at least do them the credit to say that they were true to their own instincts. Some of the very members of the present Administration were in favor of disunion. They were not only in favor of disunion, but the present Secretary of State, in a speech which he delivered a few months previous to the inauguration of Mr. Lincoln, drew a glowing picture of the progress and destiny of the two Republics. The North was to extend its dominions to a point somewhere near the region of the North Pole; while the South, in its progress of annexation, was to absorb Mexico, and, if we mistake not, its extreme southern boundary was to be only limited by the land of fire—the Terra del Fuego of the Western Hemisphere. We wonder if that is really the end that both he and the President have in view by the prosecution of this Abolition war.

Stephen A. Douglas, in the great anti-war speech which he delivered in the United States Senate on the 15th of March, 1861, the last official act of his life, made use of the following language:

> *War is disunion.* War *is final, eternal separation.* * * * * I have too much respect for any man that has standing enough to be elected a Senator, to believe that he is for war, as a means for preserving the Union. I have too much respect for his intellect to believe, for one moment, *that there is a man for war who is not a disunionist per se.* Hence I do not mean, if I can prevent it, that the enemies of the Union—*men plotting to destroy it—shall drag this country into war under the pretext of protecting the public property, and enforcing the laws, and collecting revenue, when their object is disunion and war the means of accomplishing a cherished purpose.* * * *
>
> *Peace is the only policy that can save the country.* Let peace be proclaimed as the policy, and you will find that a thrill of joy will animate the heart of every patriot in the land; confidence will be restored; business will be revived; joy will gladden every heart; bonfires will blaze upon the hill-tops and in the valleys, and the church bells will proclaim the glad tidings in every city, town, and village in America, and the applause of a grateful people will greet you everywhere. *Proclaim the policy of war, and there will be gloom and sadness and despair pictured upon the face of every patriot in the land. A war of kindred, family, and friends; father against son, mother against daughter, brother against brother, to subjugate one half of this country into obedience to the other half; if you do not mean this, if you mean peace, let this be adopted, and give the President the opportunity, through the Secretary of* War, *to speak the word "peace;" and thirty million of people will bless him with their prayers and honor him with their shouts of joy.*

But the late Mr. Douglas did not stand alone in his opinion with regard to the effects and consequences of a civil war, for we find that exactly five days before he delivered this speech in the Senate, the present Secretary of State, William H. Seward—he, whose higher law and irrepressible-conflict doctrines have aided in bringing such untold woes upon the country—he, the chief adviser of the President—addressed a letter to Mr. Adams, United States Minister to England, from which we take the following extract:

For these reasons he (the President) could not be disposed TO REJECT A CARDINAL DOGMA OF THEIRS (the seceding States)—namely, that the Federal Government COULD NOT REDUCE THE SECEDING STATES TO OBEDIENCE BY CONQUEST, EVEN ALTHOUGH HE WAS DISPOSED TO QUESTION THE PROPOSITION. BUT IN FACT THE PRESIDENT WILLINGLY ACCEPTS IT AS TRUE. ONLY AN IMPERIAL OR DESPOTIC GOVERNMENT COULD HAVE THE RIGHT TO SUBJUGATE DISAFFECTED AND INSURRECTIONARY STATES. THIS FEDERAL REPUBLICAN SYSTEM OF OURS IS, OF ALL FORMS OF GOVERNMENT, THE VERY ONE WHICH IS MOST UNFITTED FOR SUCH A LABOR.

Now, when it is understood that the letter from which we make this extract was written ONE DAY BEFORE THE BOMBARDMENT OF FORT SUMTER, it becomes at once a matter of surprise how the country was ever plunged into the present disastrous and melancholy conflict. With a Secretary of State who insisted that the President "could not be disposed to reject a cardinal dogma of theirs (the seceding States), that the Federal Government could not reduce the seceding States to obedience by conquest"—with this admission from the chief official adviser of the President, is it not extraordinary how we ever plunged, or were plunged, into this inhuman, this fratricidal war? However, the Administration itself will have to answer one of these days to the people for the manner in which it has discharged its trust.

For our own part, we have always regarded the Union as a Union of *free-will, and not of force*, and we never entertained any other thought but that the attempt to weld together its broken fragments with the sword would render its restoration impossible. Nay, more, we never believed, and *we defy any one to prove to us, either from the Constitution or from the writings of the great statesmen of the Revolution*, that there is any authority for bringing back by military force any seceding States. To be sure, there is a power inherent in the Government for the suppression of insurrection; but as Alexander Hamilton said in the convention held in New York for the ratification of the Constitution of the United States: "It must be utterly repugnant to this Constitution to subvert the State Governments or oppress the people. The coercion of States is one of the maddest projects that was ever devised. This being the case, can we suppose it wise to hazard a civil war? It would be a nation at war with itself."

This was the language of a man who loved his country. Such a thing as coercion he regarded with abhorrence, for "it would be a nation at war with itself." What a fearful departure has taken place from the principles that governed the nation in his time! We have indeed fallen on gloomy days. We have no statesman to whom the country can look in this its day of peril and disaster.

But, courage! Let us not forget the lessons of the past; let us not ignore the political teachings of the men of the Revolution; and if Abolitionism has destroyed the old Union, let us resolve at least to live at peace on the same continent with the brave men of the South whom we were once proud to call our fellow-citizens; for between them and us, despite the memories of this melancholy war, there should be none but that fraternity of feeling which has its origin in a common ancestry, a common language, and a common destiny.

The return of peace will bring with it the return of better feelings, and even if we should not have the old Union restored, the natural instincts which bind even the lower order of animals together in defense against a common enemy, will in time bring about an alliance between the North and South against the intrigues and encroachments of foreign powers upon this continent, that will, let us trust, eventually lead to a more permanent Union than that which the Abolitionists have destroyed.

MODEL RESOLUTIONS FOR THE LOYAL LEAGUERS.

(*From the* METROPOLITAN RECORD, *April* 25, 1863.)

As these patriots are now manifesting their courage in behalf of the Union, not on the battle-field, but on the bloodless rostrum, they should receive all the assistance possible to enable them to carry on their arduous labors. We have endeavored to give them some in preparing the following resolutions, which we humbly present for their acceptance, with the simple request that they be read at the next mass meeting held in the city of New York:

Whereas, It is impossible to end this war in two years with the comparatively insignificant force which we have had at different times of fifteen hundred thousand men and the fifteen hundred millions already spent; and

Whereas, There is a militia force of nearly four million of men in the free States yet to be sacrificed to Abolition designs and policy; and

Whereas, If we can carry out the Conscription Bill without opposition, we may finally succeed in establishing a military despotism; and

Whereas, Finding it impossible to subjugate the South, we must try how far we can succeed in our efforts to subjugate the North; and

Whereas, Republicanism is played out, the people having shown a willingness to submit to every species of tyranny; and

Whereas, The soldiers got the better of the citizens in Connecticut, succeeded in driving them away from the polls in Indianapolis, and have destroyed several newspaper offices throughout the country; and

Whereas, If the principles of the Constitution are ever permitted to prevail, our future prospects are particularly gloomy; and

Whereas, If the worst comes to the worst, we have made enough out of war speculations to live magnificently in foreign lands; and

Whereas, We don't care a straw for a union with slaveholders; and

Whereas, The irrepressible conflict and higher-law doctrines form the only political creed worth supporting; and

Whereas, We must play upon the feelings of the Irish people, and take advantage of their national animosity toward England by threatening a war with that country which we never intend to go into; and

Whereas, Consulting the interests of our faithful friends, the shoddy contractors, and the numerous other classes who are making money by this war, we must carry it on as long as we can; and

Whereas, We are determined to do all we can to prevent a reunion by burning down towns, sacking churches, inciting negroes to insurrection, violating the most sacred guarantees of the Constitution, ignoring the memories of the past, confiscating the property of Southern born men, threatening to overthrow every right dear to American citizens, making slaves of those who have gloried in the proud title of freemen, forcing the negroes from the slavery of the South into the Northern atmosphere of social prejudice, driving the Western States into a position of antagonism with the Union, converting the forts built for the defense of the country into prisons for the incarceration of American citizens, making the Republic a mockery in the eyes of the world, flinging discredit on, and creating distrust in, the principle of self-government: therefore,

Resolved, That we shall require the whole four millions of men who compose the militia of the Free States to be conscripted for the overthrow of slavery, and it may be "the twin evil of Popery," the suppression of the freedom of the Press, the establishment of military plantations in the South—when we conquer it—the subjugation of the North, *when the proper time comes*, the establishment of a monarchy on the ruins of the Republic, and the consolidation of the sovereign States after the overthrow of State Rights.

Resolved, That we must, by hook or by crook, carry out the Conscription, by either wheedling or bribing the Governors of those States who are supposed to be opposed to it; and to secure this end, that no money shall be spared, no Constitutional rights regarded, and no conscientious scruples observed.

Resolved, That as the South can not be subdued by our policy, the North must; and that to save ourselves from the penalty which will surely fall upon us, if we don't succeed in this conspiracy against a free people, we must establish a permanent military despotism.

Resolved, That as the people submitted with some degree of tameness to the invasion of their rights and privileges, by portions of the soldiery whom we selected for the work, they will most probably yield upon the application of a due amount of force to the conversion of the Republic into a monarchy.

Resolved, That as the first law of Nature is the law of self-preservation, and as every one of the members of the Administration, and the officials who have acted as our tools, most probably will be seized as political criminals for having violated the rights of citizenship, we must prevent such a catastrophe by continuing to hold the power in our own hands.

Resolved, That the "irrepressible conflict" shall continue between the Administration and the People, and that the "higher law" is our own will, from which there must be no appeal.

Resolved, That we shall induce, by our usual duplicity and scheming, our Irish fellow-citizens to enlist, under the idea that we intend to have a war with England, and that when they shall have been victimized to Abolitionism, we shall refuse their orphans any assistance whatever, even a roof to shelter them from the winter's cold or the summer's heat; and finally

Resolved, That we shall never be satisfied till we spend all the money we have got, that we know no North, no South, no East, no West—nothing but ourselves—that it is all nonsense to complain about sacking churches, burning down towns, or persuading negroes to massacre white people including women and children; that we shall continue the same policy to the end; that we will, if we can, let the army loose upon Northern cities and Northern homes; that we shall create anarchy, if possible, the better to secure the permanency of a military despotism, and that we shall leave no effort untried, no power with which we have been invested unemployed, no portion of the vast military and pecuniary means with which we have been intrusted unexpended, to break down that vital element of American liberty called State sovereignty, and which is the only "lion in the path" to our absolute dominion.

These resolutions we make over to the Loyal League for their special use and benefit on the simple condition that they be read at their next mass meeting in the city of New York, and also that they be published in the so-called loyal papers of the country.

WHAT THE WAR IS CARRIED ON FOR.

(*From the* METROPOLITAN RECORD, *May* 2, 1863.)

FOR the furtherance of Abolition designs.

For the permanent disruption of the Union, and the perpetuation of sectional hatred between the North and the South.

For the special benefit of the shoddy aristocracy, army and navy contractors, and all that class that wax fat and wealthy as the country grows poor, and that count their gains by the prolongation of the war.

For the establishment of a national debt equal to, if not greater than, that of England, and on which the people will have to pay a much heavier rate of interest. It may be parenthetically remarked that serious doubts are entertained whether this debt will ever be paid, as it is believed by some that the nation will eventually become bankrupt.

For the particular advantage of the New England States, whose manufacturing profits multiply as the agricultural profits of the West diminish.

For the overthrow of the State sovereignty, and the consolidation and conversion of the Republic into a military empire.

For the abrogation of constitutional rights and privileges, and for the final overthrow of liberty in the New World.

For the criminal purpose of emancipating over three millions of slaves and placing them in a social condition, which experience has shown must lead to the eventual extinction of the colored population in some localities, and their reduction to a state of vagrancy in others.

For the impoverishment of the laboring classes, and the final overthrow of universal suffrage by military force, of which we have already had a foretaste in the case of the late election at Indianapolis, when bands of soldiers drove the citizens from the polls.

For the destruction of towns and villages and the pillaging of sacred edifices, *a la* Jacksonville and Fernandina, Florida, and Winchester, Virginia.

For the degradation of the principle of self-government in the eyes of the world, and to render Republicanism a mockery and a scorn among monarchists.

For the utter annihilation of the Constitution, which has been stigmatized as "a league with Death and a covenant with Hell."

For the complete prostration of the country, so as to render it an easy prey to the diplomacy and intrigue of European statesmen.

For the retention of dictatorial power in the hands of the present Government, under the plea of military necessity afforded by the prolongation of the war.

To avert those penalties which the return of peace may be the means of inflicting upon all who have violated the great charter of American liberties.

For the purpose of showing with what success the monarchical principle of coercion can be applied to independent and sovereign States, and that the easiest way to destroy the Federal Union, which was established *by the free consent* of its constituent parts, is by the application of military force.

To prove to the world (what required no proof) that an Administration which had its origin in the spirit of disunion can never restore the Union.

A NEW JOKE.—IS IT THE PRESIDENT'S?

(*From the* METROPOLITAN RECORD, *May* 2, 1863.)

OUR readers are, of course, aware that the telegraph is under complete Government control, and nothing in the form of news can be sent by it without first passing under official inspection. Now it is also a fact that this otherwise harmless means of communication has, since it passed into new hands, become considerably corrupted by *evil communications*. Thus, it was made to inform the public at various times that the North had gained a number of decisive victories, but it almost invariably turned out that victory in these cases was but another name for defeat.

We are of the opinion that not only Mr. Lincoln's subordinates have had to do with the telegraph, but that he has absolutely been manipulating the instrument himself; for we have noticed a sort of Presidential jocularity in some of the dispatches, the paternity of which can hardly be doubted. We know—the world knows—how the Chief Magistrate contrives to keep up his spirits in the midst of difficulties that would have overwhelmed the jocund nature of Mark Tapley himself—and we recollect a story that was told of his having called upon one of the officers during a visit to the bloody field of Antietam to sing for him "Jim along Josey," or some other spirit-stirring negro melody. We are not certain whether the officer did this, but if he did not, it was not the fault of our lively and loquacious Executive.

In olden times it was customary for the monarch to wile away his tedious hours by the droll antics and the witticisms of a court fool. The ever-flowing humor and inexhaustible fund of jokes possessed by the sixteenth magistrate of the United States renders what was an indispensable adjunct to the court of olden times entirely unnecessary at the White House, for the principal occupant of the Presidential mansion is a sort of dual character, and so saves the Nation the expense of supporting a jester.

But we are forgetting the telegraphic joke; and as our readers may be somewhat impatient to see it, here it is as it comes over the wires:

> The rebel pickets informed ours that they had a new general on their side who treats the army with great severity. On inquiring his name, they replied—General Starvation.

What do our readers think of that? If that is not in every way worthy of the last successor of Washington, we are no judge of a Presidential *hit.*

Is there no publisher sufficiently enterprising to collect all the witticisms, all the puns, and all the anecdotes of the Executive, and give them to the world in an imperishable form? It strikes us that Barnum is just the man to undertake the task; or the incumbent of the Presidential chair himself, when he gets through with the cares of Government, and descends to the ranks of private life, might profitably devote his leisure hours to the agreeable work. Such a book, issued under the title of *Lincolniana*, would, we have no doubt, have an immense run, almost as great a run as that made by the President himself into Washington some two years ago, under cover of a Scotch cap and military cloak.

THE ABOLITION POLICY OF THE ADMINISRATION, AND WHAT IT HAS ACCOMPLISHED.

(*From the* METROPOLITAN RECORD, *May* 2, 1863.)

THAT Abolitionism has been the cause of the present condition of the country is a fact which we think no rational man will deny. There are many, however, who insist, in the very face of history itself, and in utter defiance of the most solemn and repeated asseverations of the greatest statesmen of the country, that to Slavery is attributable all the calamities with which the nation is now afflicted. There might be some ground for this assertion were the peculiar institution a thing of recent origin—were it introduced into the country after, instead of before the Revolution. But when we find that the very men who framed the Declaration of Independence, and who pledged their lives, their fortunes, and their sacred honor to the support and maintenance of American freedom, were themselves slaveholders, holding slaves to the hour of their death, and then, at that dread hour, transmitting their proprietary interest in them to their natural heirs—there is not even a shadow of foundation on which such an assertion could rest. It is clearly, then, a fabrication—an invention; and upon this invention has, strange to say, been built up a party that has shaken the Republic to its very foundations, leaving to the world nothing but the melancholy ruins of its former greatness. While the Constitution guaranteed the peculiar institution against the assaults of this factious sectional party—while conservative Congresses passed laws which were considered necessary to fortify, as it were, the provisions of the Constitution—this party, acting through its various cliques, either denounced that instrument as "a league with death and a covenant with hell," or sought its nullification through the advocacy and enforcement of the "irrepressible conflict" and "higher-law" doctrines. Urged on, in its mad, fanatical career, by a hatred as bitter against the people of the South as against Slavery, it omitted no opportunity through the press, the pulpit, the rostrum, and through the various influences of social life, to stigmatize our Southern fellow-countrymen as criminals both in the eyes of God and man. It held them up to the odium of the civilized world as men who were unworthy of Christian fellowship. It violated the compact by which the States were held together by securing the passage of Personal Liberty Bills in the Legislatures of Northern States; it organized "underground railroads" for the purpose of *stealing* away Southern property; it concocted the raid of John Brown and his fellow-murderers into the first State of the Union, the glorious old commonwealth of Virginia; it leagued itself with the English enemies of the Republic, and accepted the ever-ready donations of British gold to strengthen the blows which it aimed at the life of the country.

What cared the men of which this party is composed for the sacrifices that were made by the patriots of the Revolution to build up the Union? what cared they for the freedom of white men so long as their perverted sympathy could find an object for its exercise in an inferior race? What cared they for the physical sufferings and destitution of thousands of their own color at home and within easy reach, so long as the sable sons of Africa were to be elevated to a state of freedom for which they were never designed by nature, and to which, with a rare exception, they had no aspirations? What cared they for all this? They were bent upon the overthrow of Slavery, although the warning voice of the great statesmen of the Republic was raised in deprecation of their fiendish designs. How far they have succeeded in their fell purpose let the Abolition Administration at Washington answer. But it is said that the President and his Cabinet do not represent the extreme section of the Abolition party; that they are constitutional and law-abiding men; that their chief aim has been to administer the affairs of the country on a national, and not on a partisan or sectional basis. Now, we venture to say, and we shall sustain our statements with irrefragable testimony, that there is not a particle of truth in any portion of this defense; that it is false in its inception, false in its utterance, and false in every word and line—in a word, that it is as false to truth as the hearts in which it was conceived are false to the spirit of the Union.

No sooner was their candidate duly installed in the Presidential chair than he revealed his policy by the appointment of Abolitionists as his Cabinet councilors. The first was his present Secretary of State, whose opposition to Slavery was notorious, while acting as a Senator of the Union. In a speech which he made in the Senate, March 11, 1850, Mr. Seward absolutely threatened the Southern States with civil war in the event of their continued opposition to emancipation. He said:

"When this answer shall be given, it will appear that the question of dissolving the Union is a complex question; that it embraces the fearful issue whether the Union shall stand, and Slavery, under the steady, peaceful action of moral, social, and political causes, be removed by gradual, voluntary efforts, and with compensation, or whether THE UNION SHALL BE DISSOLVED, AND CIVIL WARS ENSUE, BRINGING ON VIOLENT BUT COMPLETE AND IMMEDIATE EMANCIPATION. We are now arrived at that stage when that crisis can be foreseen, when we must foresee it. It is directly before us. Its shadow is upon us."

So much for the Secretary of State, and let us add that we could fill column after column with proofs of as strong a character in regard to his Abolition tendencies and policy. But we shall give another extract, and this we take from a speech delivered also in the Senate, but six years later, April 9th, 1856. On this occasion he made use of the following remarkable language:

"The solemnity of the occasion draws over our heads that cloud of disunion which must always arise whenever the subject of Slavery is agitated. Still the debate goes on, more ardently, earnestly, and angrily than ever before. It employs now not merely logic, reproach, menace, retort, and defiance, BUT SABERS, RIFLES, AND CANNON. * * Then the Free States and Slave States of the Atlantic, divided and warring with each other, would disgust the Free States of the Pacific, and THEY WOULD HAVE ABUNDANT CAUSE AND JUSTIFICATION FOR WITHDRAWING FROM A UNION PRODUCTIVE NO LONGER OF PEACE, SAFETY, AND LIBERTY TO THEMSELVES, and no longer holding up the cherished hopes of mankind."

Did it never occur to the present Secretary of State that he and his fellow-Abolitionists were giving to the South "*abundant cause and justification for withdrawing from a Union productive no longer of peace, safety, and liberty to themselves?*"

It is unnecessary to furnish any evidence in regard to the Abolition character of the other members of the present Administration. Their course since their installment in office should, we think, set at rest whatever doubts might have been entertained on this point. If their views and opinions do not run altogether in harmonious accord, there is certainly a wonderful unanimity of action between them. As for the President himself, it is but justice to him to say that he has been wonderfully consistent in his efforts to give practical effect to the following remarkable expression of his political faith in the future destiny of the Republic: "I BELIEVE THIS GOVERNMENT CAN NOT ENDURE PERMANENTLY HALF SLAVE AND HALF FREE."

Impressed with this belief, he took a solemn oath to faithfully execute the duties of his office, and to preserve, protect, and defend the Constitution of the United States. Strange contradiction; although there are some who would call it by a harsher term, and who would perhaps insist that he has made use of the power intrusted to him to fulfill his assertion, that "this Government can not endure permanently half slave and half free." Without stopping at this point to argue the matter with those who entertain such a belief as to the designs of the Chief Magistrate, we propose to present a brief review of the principal acts of his Administration during the two years that have elapsed since his inauguration. In the first place, then, his selection of leading Abolitionists as his Cabinet councilors was, to our mind, a striking indication of the course which he intended to pursue.

He has been in their hands from the very first, and he has been their instrument in the indorsement of every legislative act aimed by the last Congress at the perpetuity of the "peculiar institution." Not a single measure originated with him, or received his encouragement, looking toward conciliation and compromise with the South. They were offered no terms but those contained in a Constitution whose guarantees had been violated again and again, and whose obligations exercised no restraining force upon the very men who claimed to act under its authority. Then, too, with what indecent haste his fellow-Abolitionists in Congress passed the bill abolishing Slavery in the District of Columbia. A Congress which did not represent even two thirds of the Union; and with what uncomplaining resignation he took up his Presidential pen, and, placing his signature thereto, gave it all the form and character of a law.

But the President did not stop here; he must needs go further to add fuel to the flames that were fast enveloping the nation. He must insult and worry the Border Slave States that still remained in the Union, with propositions for compensated emancipation, and that, too, before he ever consulted the wishes of the country on the subject, before he ever took means to ascertain whether the people of the free States were willing to be taxed to secure the freedom of a race which is unfitted by nature for its exercise in the same community with white men. Now came the Confiscation Bill, which was another blow aimed by the dominant Abolition faction against the constitutional securities that had been wisely thrown around the "peculiar institution" in a spirit of patriotic legislation. That bill was designed to deprive Southern men of their slave property, and was as unjustifiable and unconstitutional as the arbitrary acts of the Administration in suppressing freedom of speech and the liberty of the press, in the incarceration of Northern citizens, and in the conduct of authorized official burglars in the invasion of the home sanctuary, and the plunder, for the so-called use of the Government, of the letters and private documents of the free citizens of this Republic.

The record of Administrative acts also tells us how the boundaries of a sovereign State were broken down, and how a new State was established therein, without regard to the sovereignty of the people, or an effort being made to get their concurrence in the act. We need hardly say, however, that the admission of Kanawha into the Union is a farce; that it has no binding force, and that the outrage perpetrated upon the Constitution, upon State sovereignty, and upon popular rights, will one day recoil with fearful effect upon the heads of the men by whom the vile deed was perpetrated.

But the crowning act of an Abolition despotism was that set forth in the Emancipation Proclamation, by which, with the stroke of a pen, the President attempted to destroy the property of a portion of the country, amounting to between two and three thousand millions of dollars. This was called a military measure, and it is remarkabl to what extent the military power has taken the place of the civil in this Republican government of ours. Over three millions of slaves were, by this act, to be forced from the possession of their masters into a new condition of life, for which their previous habits and pursuits, as well as their own nature, disqualified them. Over three millions of this class of beings were to be flung in a helpless state upon the country, having been previously divorced from the only state in which their labor could be made productive and of value to tens of millions of the superior race all over the world. What, let us ask, has become of those who have been emancipated? Have they not been supported at the expense of the Government, or rather at the expense of the people? and when this Administration shall have passed out of office, who can prevent these emancipated negroes from lapsing into a state of vagrancy?

There are many other facts to which we could refer in proof of the Abolition course and policy of the authorities at Washington, but those we have given will, we think, suffice for the present. And now, is any man so stupid or so wanting in common intelligence as not to see that it is impossible for such an Administration to restore the Union? Does any man believe that the further prosecution of the war under such auspices, or, in fact, under any auspices, could bring back the South? On the contrary, is it not evident that the restoration of the Union through such an agency is a hopeless prospect? No Conscription Bill can over accomplish such a result. *The thing has gone too far;* the Administration has lost its power, and we venture to say that it is at the present time in a state of trepidation and nervousness that shows the weakness to which it has been reduced by its own acts. *At this mo-*

ment the Governor of New York occupies a stronger position than that of the President of the United States. He can call out the militia of the Empire State—can the President of the United States do that without his permission? He represents a *majority* of the citizens of this great State—what portion of the people, outside of the Abolition faction, and contractors and office-holders, does President Lincoln represent? Can he even say that he is now carrying on the war at the desire of a majority of the people? Let the recent State elections answer. What, then, is this war carried on for? Why are hundreds of thousands more called for? Has the human holocaust offered at the shrine of fanaticism not satisfied the Abolition cry for "more blood," and must the conscription be enforced to add to the number of victims? The country is weary and sick of this work of slaughter—this aimless butchery of its people. It must come to an end some time, and that time should be now. We can not afford to have the industrial ranks of the country further decimated by this Abolition crusade, to have the great army of widows and orphans still further increased by new accessions, to have the trade and commerce of the country depressed still more by war's paralyzing influence, and to have the great laboring classes ground down to the earth by excessive taxation.

THE STATESMEN OF THE REVOLUTION ON THE RIGHT OF COERCION.

(*From the* METROPOLITAN RECORD, *May* 9, 1863.)

WE have all along contended that the Constitution conferred no right or authority for the coercion of States, and we now insist that the great statesmen by whom that instrument was framed deprecated the employment of military force against refractory States. This great and important fact has, however, been completely lost sight of in the terrible controversy by which the country is at present convulsed. The people appear to have forgotten the lessons of the Revolution; they have been carried away by the material prosperity to which the country has attained, and in their pursuit of worldly gain have neglected the study of those principles which gave birth to the Union. Despite our common-school education, and the opportunities afforded for the acquisition of knowledge by the vast multiplication of books of all kinds, we are, as a people, wofully ignorant of the Constitution, the circumstances under which it was adopted, and the biographies of the great men with whom it originated. But for this ignorance, for which there is no excuse, the Abolitionists would never have succeeded in destroying the Union; and but for this ignorance, also, there could be no alienation of feeling between the North and the South. It is, however, urged that if all this could have been prevented by a better knowledge of constitutional principles, that it is now too late to discuss the question as to which of the two great sections of the country is right—the North or the South. We understand fully the spirit which would dispose of the matter in this way. It is that spirit which blindly insists upon a continuance in wrong-doing, even with a full acknowledgment of the offense. It is that obstinate persistence in error which has destroyed nations as well as individuals, and which can have but one, and that a fatal, termination. We shall never willingly yield an acquiescence in the ruinous policy which springs from such a principle. We do not believe in giving way to it in the first instance, or in the second instance, or in the last instance; and we shall continue, therefore, to protest against it to the end.

Let us, then, repeat that we find no authority either in the Constitution or in the writings of its authors for the employment of coercion in the case of a State seceding from the Union. On the contrary, whatever we find upon the subject in these writings is directly in conflict even with the assumption of such a right on the part of the General Government. There could not be anything clearer or more forcible than their statements on this point. How the authorities at Washington could have fallen into any error regarding the power with which they are invested is something extraordinary. The Secretary of State can not certainly lay claim to exemption in the matter, for, as we proved in the RECORD of April 25, he expressed the belief that the United States Government had no authority to coerce States which had arrayed themselves in opposition thereto. Writing to Mr. Adams almost on the eve of the attack on Fort Sumter, he said:

> "ONLY AN IMPERIAL OR DESPOTIC GOVERNMENT COULD HAVE THE RIGHT TO SUBJUGATE DISAFFECTED AND INSURRECTIONARY STATES. THIS FEDERAL REPUBLICAN SYSTEM OF OURS IS THE VERY ONE WHICH IS MOST UNFITTED FOR SUCH A LABOR."

It is evident from this that the Secretary of State is fully conversant with the opinions of the Fathers of the Republic on this much-vexed but clearly defined question. We referred on a former occasion to the remarkably forcible manner in which Alexander Hamilton expressed himself upon this vital matter, and we shall take the liberty of reproducing his language at this time. It will be remembered that the occasion on which it was elicited was during a debate held in the New York Convention for the ratification of the Constitution of the United States:

> "THE COERCION OF STATES," said Hamilton, "IS ONE OF THE MADDEST PROJECTS THAT WAS EVER DEVISED. A FAILURE OF COMPLIANCE WILL NEVER BE CONFINED TO A SINGLE STATE. THIS BEING THE CASE, CAN WE SUPPOSE IT WISE TO HAZARD A CIVIL WAR? IT WOULD BE A NATION AT WAR WITH ITSELF. CAN ANY REASONABLE MAN BE WELL DISPOSED TOWARD A GOVERNMENT THAT MAKES WAR AND CARNAGE THE ONLY MEANS OF SUPPORTING ITSELF—A GOVERNMENT THAT CAN EXIST ONLY BY THE SWORD? EVERY SUCH WAR MUST INVOLVE THE INNOCENT WITH THE GUILTY. THIS SINGLE CONSIDERATION SHOULD NOT BE INEFFICIENT TO DISPOSE EVERY PEACEABLE CITIZEN AGAINST SUCH A GOVERNMENT."

Such was the belief entertained and expressed by a statesman who certainly could not be accused of too strong a leaning toward political latitudinarianism. He shrank from the very contemplation of coercion "as repugnant to the Constitution," "as one of the maddest projects that was ever devised," and added, that "as every such war must involve the innocent with the guilty, *this single consideration should dispose every peaceable citizen against such a government.*"

We now turn from Alexander Hamilton to James Madison, another prominent member of the Convention that framed the Constitution, and we may add, one of the great statesmen with whom that important document originated. It is hardly to be supposed that he did not thoroughly understand its character, and the authority and powers with which it invested the Government in its relations toward the States. And yet no man could be more emphatic in his denunciation of the mere idea that the Federal Government had a right to coerce a State by military force. Let all who have insisted on the invasion and subjugation of the South, and the vigorous prosecution of the war, read what Madison said at the Convention which gave the present Constitution to the States for adoption :

"THE MORE I REFLECT ON THE USE OF FORCE, THE MORE I DOUBT THE PRACTICABILITY AND EFFICIENCY OF IT WHEN APPLIED TO A PEOPLE COLLECTIVELY. THE USE OF AN ARMED FORCE AGAINST A DISOBEDIENT STATE, OR STATES, WOULD LOOK MORE LIKE A DECLARATION OF WAR THAN AN INFLICTION OF PUNISHMENT, AND WOULD BE RIGHTLY CONSIDERED A DISSOLUTION OF THE PREVIOUS COMPACTS BY WHICH IT MIGHT BE BOUND. THE MOST JARRING ELEMENTS, FIRE AND WATER, ARE NOT MORE INCOMPATIBLE THAN SUCH A STRANGE MIXTURE OF CIVIL LIBERTY AND MILITARY EXECUTION. WILL THE MILITIA MARCH FROM ONE STATE TO ANOTHER FOR THE PURPOSE OF COERCION? IF THEY DO, WILL NOT THE CITIZENS OF INVADED STATES ASSIST ONE ANOTHER UNTIL THEY RISE AS ONE MAN, AND SHAKE OFF WHAT THEY WILL DENOUNCE AS THE HATED UNION ALTOGETHER? IF YOU SUBJUGATE THEM, HOW ARE YOU TO HOLD THEM UNDER A CONSTITUTION THAT IS TO BE IMPOSED TO INSURE DOMESTIC TRANQUILLITY AND PROMOTE THE GENERAL WELFARE?"

When we reflect on the character and the high position held by Madison in the confidence of the people, and his great ability as a statesman, we can hardly suppose that he gave utterance to these opinions on the subject of coercion without serious reflection and consideration. Then it must be borne in mind that he was, so to speak, a member of the Government himself, and, in his official capacity, pledged to its support and maintenance. Such being the case, it will not do to treat his statements lightly, or as of little moment. But let us analyze his language and see if there can be any misconception in regard to the meaning which he intended to convey.

In the first place, then, he speaks of the use of force, as applied to a people in their collective capacity, that is, in the organized form of a State or States. Upon that point we think there can be no doubt whatever. Next, it is essential to understand the circumstances under which he doubts the practicability and efficiency of this force. But there can be no conjecture on this point either; it is of a DISOBEDIENT STATE OR STATES he speaks. And then he goes on to say that the employment of an armed force in this case "would look more like a declaration of war than an infliction of punishment;" and WHAT FOLLOWS—mark this emphatic declaration from one of the authors of the Constitution—"WOULD BE RIGHTLY CONSIDERED A DISSOLUTION OF THE PREVIOUS COMPACTS BY WHICH IT MIGHT BE BOUND."

Here, then, is James Madison insisting, as Stephen A. Douglas in his last speech in the United States Senate asserted, that civil war is disunion—nay, not only insisting that it is disunion, but that the employment of armed force against a disobedient State "would be rightly considered a dissolution of the previous compacts by which it might be bound." After this declaration, he puts the case still stronger by this remarkably expressive illustration: "The most jarring elements, fire and water, are not more incompatible than such a strange mixture of civil liberty and military execution." Is the English language capable of stronger expression than this? Could the subject be put more clearly or more forcibly? We should like to hear what construction the Loyal Leaguers, and those who are in favor of a vigorous prosecution of the war, would put upon the language of James Madison. If it is capable of another interpretation, then we should like to see it. After giving his views on the right of coercion, Madison then proceeds to set forth the result of such a policy; and it is really remarkable to see how far his predictions have been fulfilled by the present war. He asks: "Will the militia march from one State to another for the purpose of coercion?" and then adds, "if they do, WILL NOT THE CITIZENS OF INVADED STATES ASSIST ONE ANOTHER, UNTIL THEY RISE AS ONE MAN AND SHAKE OFF WHAT THEY WILL DENOUNCE AS THE HATED UNION ALTOGETHER."

With the clear perception of a great statesman, Madison foresaw the results of the policy of coercion, and warned his countrymen against employing it as a means of preserving the Union. His foresight in this case is so remarkable, that one would imagine he was writing subsequent to the events instead of prophesying in regard to them three quarters of a century before their occurrence.

How comes it that we have gone so far astray from the landmarks of the Revolution? How comes it that we have forgotten the teachings of the fathers of the Republic? What *ignis fatuus* has lured us from the straight path which they marked out? The country has been seduced from its political faith and principles by the foul spirit of discord in the form of Abolitionism. We have given up George Washington, James Madison, Alexander Hamilton, and their compatriots of the Revolution, for such men as Abraham Lincoln, John C. Fremont, Charles Sumner, and their fellow-Abolitionists, who have told us that the Union could not exist half slave half free. We have abandoned the traditionary policy of the country, which was that of compromise, for the law of force and coercion. *We have made war upon State Governments*, and the Administration, in doing so, HAS BEEN GUILTY OF THE MOST FLAGRANT OUTRAGE UPON THAT VERY PRINCIPLE OF AUTHORITY BY WHICH IT IS SUSTAINED. Its whole spirit in the present crisis has been in direct conflict with the interests of the country. Its policy in the prosecution of the war has been more calculated to widen the chasm that now divides the North and the South, than to heal the wounds of our bleeding country. Its policy is the policy of rapine, plunder, and devastation. Abundant proofs of this have been furnished by the reports of recent raids in Southern States, when private property was destroyed with the most ruthless vandalism; the homes of planters were burned to the ground; towns and villages were given over to the brand, and even sacred edifices were not exempted from the general destruction; and all this was done in sovereign and independent States, and by men who boasted their inheritance of the principles of civil and religious liberty. The work of confiscation and emancipation has only been stayed by the bravery of a people who firmly believed in the righteousness of their cause, and who now stand upon the same ground with regard to State rights that was occupied by James Madison, Alexander Hamilton, and the other patriots of the Revolution.

There is no disguising the fact, that this is an Abolition war; that it is carried on by men who have worked all their lives for the dissolution of the Union. They may try to conceal their policy, but the facts are on record against them, and they can not escape the crushing evidence of their own words and deeds. They have a fearful account to answer for. They have sacrificed a nation to a sentiment; they have plunged the land in a sea of blood; they have brought desolation and mourning into tens of thousands of once happy homes; they have combined with the British Abolitionists for the overthrow of the Republic; hundreds of thousands of our people have been victimized to their fiendish designs, and they have struck a blow at popular liberty from which it may never recover. Must we plunge irretrievably in the abyss which has been opened by the fell spirit of *Abolitionism?* Must we continue this shedding of brothers' blood, this work of Cain in a more extended and fearful form? Are the votaries of Moloch not yet satisfied, and must they have more blood? Forbid it every sense of right, every sense of justice, every sense of humanity. Let us then have peace, that the wounds of the country may be healed. Let us have peace, that the tears of the widows and orphans may cease to flow Let us have peace, that an end may be put to the military despotism under which the people are now groaning. Let us have peace, that the country may not be overburdened with excessive taxation. Let us have peace, as the only means of averting the reign of anarchy which will surely attend the prolongation of this war. And let us have peace if we would not have American freedom crushed out by the heel of an armed despotism.

THE SOVEREIGNTY OF THE STATES.

(*From the* METROPOLITAN RECORD, *May* 16, 1863.)

THE desperate effort that is being made by the Administration to overthrow the sovereignty of the States and to establish a consolidated despotism on its ruins has been practically illustrated by the establishment of the bogus State of Kanawha. If the Administration had placed no other fact on record but this, it would have been sufficient to have consigned it to everlasting infamy. That act was not only an insult to the sovereignty of every State, but it was a deadly blow aimed at the liberty of the whole country. The miserable and mendacious tricksters at Washington, in all their despotic policy, have not committed a more despotic act than that by which a new State was carved out of Virginia without the consent of the only parties by whom it could be constitutionally accomplished —its people. It was, however, only a natural sequence of the policy of the Abolition party, whose hostility to the perpetuity of the Union has been so forcibly illustrated by "the powers that be."

The division of the State of Virginia is only an example on a small scale of the dissolution of the Union. It was a violation of the very principle of unity, as well as a great outrage upon the independence of a sovereign State. Nothing is more clearly set forth in the Constitution, and the writings of the statesmen of the Revolution, than this great principle of the inviolability of a State. Yet the Administration, although relying upon the support which it has received from some of the States FOR THE SUBJUGATION OF THE OTHERS, have been steadily and persistently engaged in undermining the very foundation upon which they rest. They have carried their Abolition policy not only into Southern States, but into Northern States. They have imprisoned not only Southern citizens, but Northern citizens; and they have established military law not only in the South, but in the North. THE GOVERNMENT, THEREFORE, MAY PROPERLY BE SAID TO BE AT WAR WITH BOTH SECTIONS, for our fellow-citizens of this and other States have felt the power of its tyranny. In the State of Ohio, which has contributed over a hundred thousand volunteers, the military has superseded the civil power, and at the dead hour of night its sovereignty sustained a most serious wound by the forcible, the unconstitutional arrest of one of its most prominent citizens. It remains with the people of that State to vindicate its sovereignty and their own rights as freemen. But if they fail to do this, now that the Administration has set them at defiance, then they are unworthy of the name of Americans.

The statesmen of the Revolution were particularly emphatic in regard to State sovereignty. Indeed, so emphatic were they that they even regarded the sovereignty of a State as of more vital importance than the Union itself.

Evidences of this are to be found throughout their speeches and their writings. Alexander Hamilton, to whose writings we have on several occasions referred, made one of his most powerful speeches on this subject in the New York Convention for the ratification of the Constitution of the United States. From this speech we make the following timely and appropriate extract:

"IF THE STATE GOVERNMENTS WERE TO BE ABOLISHED, THE QUESTION WOULD WEAR A DIFFERENT FACE. BUT THIS IDEA IS INADMISSIBLE. THEY ARE ABSOLUTELY NECESSARY TO THE SYSTEM. THEIR EXISTENCE MUST FORM A LEADING PRINCIPLE IN THE MOST PERFECT CONSTITUTION WE COULD FORM. I INSIST THAT IT NEVER CAN BE THE INTEREST OR DESIRE OF THE NATIONAL LEGISLATURE TO DESTROY THE STATE GOVERNMENTS. IT CAN DERIVE NO ADVANTAGE FROM SUCH AN EVENT; BUT, ON THE CONTRARY, WOULD LOSE AN INDISPENSABLE SUPPORT, A NECESSARY AID IN EXECUTING THE LAWS, AND CONVEYING THE INFLUENCE OF GOVERNMENT TO THE DOORS OF THE PEOPLE. THE UNION IS DEPENDENT ON THE WILL OF THE STATE GOVERNMENTS FOR ITS CHIEF MAGISTRATE AND FOR ITS SENATE. THE BLOW AIMED AT THE MEMBERS MUST GIVE A FATAL WOUND TO THE HEAD; AND THE DESTRUCTION OF THE STATES MUST BE AT ONCE A POLITICAL SUICIDE. CAN THE NATIONAL GOVERNMENT BE GUILTY OF THIS MADNESS? WHAT INDUCEMENTS, WHAT TEMPTATIONS CAN THEY HAVE? WILL THEY ATTACH NEW HONORS TO THEIR STATION? WILL THEY INCREASE THE NATIONAL STRENGTH?

WILL THEY MULTIPLY THE NATIONAL RESOURCES? WILL THEY MAKE THEMSELVES MORE RESPECTABLE IN THE VIEW OF FOREIGN NATIONS OR OF THEIR FELLOW-CITIZENS BY ROBBING THE STATES OF THEIR CONSTITUTIONAL PRIVILEGES? BUT IMAGINE FOR A MOMENT THAT A POLITICAL FRENZY SHOULD SEIZE THE GOVERNMENT—SUPPOSE THEY SHOULD MAKE THE ATTEMPT. CERTAINLY, SIR, IT WOULD BE FOREVER IMPRACTICABLE. THIS HAS BEEN SUFFICIENTLY DEMONSTRATED BY REASON AND EXPERIENCE."

This great statesman tells us that the State governments are absolutely necessary to the system, from which follows the inevitable inference that the overthrow of State sovereignty must lead to its total destruction. He insisted that it could not be the interest or desire of the National Legislature to destroy the State governments; but this has been done; and it is more than probable that the Government will lose thereby "an indispensable support, a necessary aid in executing the laws, and conveying the influence of Government to the doors of the people."

He tells us that "the destruction of the States must be at once a political suicide." We believe that the Government has committed this "suicide," that, in fact, it has no longer political life, but only the semblance of vitality. The "National Government" has been "guilty of this madness," and the "inducements" and "temptations" are the consolidation of the States and the centralization of power at Washington under the control of a military despotism. This is the motive by which our "*rulers*" have been actuated. This is the political frenzy by which they have been seized. They have made the attempt to rob the States of their "constitutional privileges;" but we have the authority of Hamilton for saying that their mad scheme is "forever impracticable." The Administration may seem to triumph for a while, but that they will fail, miserably, ignominiously fail, there can be no doubt; for as the great statesman to whom we referred says, "this has been sufficiently demonstrated by reason and experience."

It is true that Hamilton never supposed the possibility of a State being employed as an instrument of coercion, as is evident from the following extract contained in his speech delivered on the occasion alluded to above:

"BUT CAN WE BELIEVE THAT ONE STATE WILL EVER SUFFER ITSELF TO BE USED AS AN INSTRUMENT OF COERCION? THE THING IS A DREAM—IT IS IMPOSSIBLE."

Such a thing as the employment of one sovereign State for the coercion of another sovereign State was regarded by him as a dream—as an impossibility. He shrank from the very contemplation of it; but then he could never conceive the probability of the elevation to power of a party which had its existence in the very spirit of disunion. Let us see, however, what he thinks of the success of an effort on the part of the General Government to carry out its plan of consolidation and centralization. We quote from one of his speeches delivered at the same convention:

"THE STATE ESTABLISHMENTS OF CIVIL AND MILITARY OFFICERS OF EVERY DESCRIPTION, INFINITELY SURPASSING IN NUMBERS ANY POSSIBLE CORRESPONDENT ESTABLISHMENTS IN THE GENERAL GOVERNMENT, WILL CREATE SUCH AN EXTENT AND COMPLICATION OF ATTACHMENTS AS WILL EVER SECURE THE PREDILECTION AND SUPPORT OF THE PEOPLE. WHENEVER, THEREFORE, CONGRESS SHALL MEDITATE ANY INFRINGEMENT OF THE STATE CONSTITUTIONS, THE GREAT BODY OF THE PEOPLE NATURALLY TAKE PART WITH THEIR DOMESTIC REPRESENTATIVES. CAN THE GENERAL GOVERNMENT WITHSTAND SUCH A UNITED OPPOSITION? WILL THE PEOPLE SUFFER THEMSELVES TO BE STRIPPED OF THEIR PRIVILEGES? WILL THEY SUFFER THEIR LEGISLATURES TO BE REDUCED TO A SHADOW AND A NAME? THE IDEA IS SHOCKING TO COMMON SENSE."

We have no doubt whatever that the Administration in its frenzy will yet provoke a conflict *with one or more of the Northern States, in which it will inevitably be overthrown.* The people in such an emergency, as Hamilton predicts, will take part with their domestic representatives, for they will not "suffer themselves to be stripped of their privileges;" they will not "suffer their legislatures to be reduced to a shadow and a name. The idea is shocking to common sense."

In a conflict between them and the General Government, the States of New York and New Jersey alone would be more than a match for all the force which it could bring against them. It is well at this time, in view of recent occurrences, to consider such a thing among the probabilities of the future, for the threatening position of the Administration toward the sovereignty of the States forebodes no good to our liberty. If the Union is ever restored, it will be through the great cardinal principle of State sovereignty. We can not set aside this principle without annihilating the Union. Let us even succeed in conquering the South by overturning State sovereignty in both sections, and we may bid a long farewell to democratic freedom. Can we afford to purchase union on such terms?

We have before referred to the writings of Alexander Hamilton on the subject of State sovereignty and the coercion of States, and we shall conclude this article with an extract from one of his letters which we find in No. 16 of the *Federalist:*

WHOEVER CONSIDERS THE POPULOUSNESS AND STRENGTH OF SEVERAL OF THESE STATES SINGLY AT THE PRESENT JUNCTURE, AND LOOKS FORWARD TO WHAT THEY WILL BECOME EVEN AT THE DISTANCE OF HALF A CENTURY, WILL AT ONCE DISMISS AS IDLE AND VISIONARY ANY SCHEME WHICH AIMS AT REGULATING THEM OR COERCING THEM IN THEIR COLLECTIVE CAPACITIES BY THE GENERAL GOVERNMENT. A PROJECT OF THIS KIND IS LITTLE LESS ROMANTIC THAN THE MONSTER-TAMING SPIRIT ATTRIBUTED TO THE FABULOUS HEROES AND DEMIGODS OF ANTIQUITY. EVEN IN THOSE CONFEDERACIES WHICH HAVE BEEN COMPOSED OF MEMBERS SMALLER THAN MANY OF OUR COUNTIES, THE PRINCIPLE OF LEGISLATION FOR SOVEREIGN STATES, SUPPORTED BY MILITARY COERCION, HAS NEVER BEEN FOUND EFFECTUAL. IT HAS RARELY BEEN ATTEMPTED TO BE EMPLOYED AGAINST THE WEAKER MEMBERS; AND IN MOST INSTANCES ATTEMPTS THUS TO COERCE THE REFRACTORY AND DISOBEDIENT HAVE BEEN THE SIGNALS OF BLOODY WARS, IN WHICH ONE HALF THE CONFEDERACY HAS DISPLAYED ITS BANNERS AGAINST THE OTHER. WE WANT NO SUCH GOVERNMENT AS THIS.

THE NORTHERN PLAGUE.

(*From the* METROPOLITAN RECORD, *May* 23, 1863.)

SOME years ago there burst forth in the North a mental and moral epidemic of a most alarming character. From the East it came, and onward it swept, sparing neither youth nor age, neither man nor woman, in its progress. Firm faith and fixed principles alone withstood it, everything else went down before it like corn before the reaper. It attacked the speaker on the stand, the writer at his desk, the preacher in the pulpit. It infected the public press, it polluted public offices, it contaminated the National Council Chamber. It was propagated by pen and tongue, by diseased imitation and morbid sympathy. Weak minds and disordered imaginations fell an easy prey to it, while those whose healthy moral condition enabled them to defy its venom stood aside, and with gloomy forebodings marked its desolating career; saw, with feelings unutterable, charity, faith, feeling, kindliness, courtesy vanish before it; saw patriotism wilted by its breadth and truth obscured by its influence. Fear fell upon them—the fear that Christians feel when souls are in peril, the fear that patriots feel when their country is in danger—when they saw nature outraged for a sentiment and religion displaced to make room for philanthropy. Philanthropy, the idol of the nineteenth century, the god of men who acknowledge no other.

Never was there such a scourge seen among men as this earth-born, or rather hell-born plague. It brought hatred and lying in its train, it brought pharisaical assumption and spiritual pride, it brought malice and uncharitableness. Whatever it touched was blighted, whatever it breathed on was smirched. Under its influence men became blasphemers, and boldly undertook to rectify the work of the Omnipotent, and to abrogate the laws of nature as if they were those of the United States. The sense of right and wrong became obscured, the capacity to judge correctly was lost, and the plague-smitten monomaniacs of the North drifted through time clinging to their one idea as the drowning wretch clings to a straw.

As physical plagues possess the power of absorbing or

destroying other diseases, so the great Northern Plague of Abolitionism gradually swallowed up every other ism. Who now hears of Fourierism, Free-loveism, Communism, *et hoc genus omne?* They are lost in Abolitionism, as affluents are in the stream they feed. Yes, the plague has reached its height; it has carried off its thousands and hundreds of thousands; it has stricken down the youth in his joyousness, and the strong man in his strength; it has made the land desolate, and it has crushed the great heart of the people. It has, devastated North and South; it has decimated East and West, and its ravages have been cruelly impartial. No sooner is the wail of agony for the loved and lost stilled in the lonely homesteads of Vermont than it rises wild and impassioned from the orange groves of Carolina. No sooner does the tide of sorrow ebb on the Atlantic shore than it flows in overwhelming force upon the golden coasts of the Pacific. Throughout that immense tract of God's earth men call the United States, it has not left one spot unvisited—scarcely one home unscathed. Enter any home unbidden and at random—mark the stooping forms and careworn faces—mark the empty seats and vacant places by the fireside; and, though no yellow flag flutters from the roof, be sure the plague has passed there, culling as it passed the brightest blossom of the hearth, and nipping the fairest bud that grew in that home garden.

If you are not one that will not learn from the eye, but only from the ear, then ask and be convinced—"Killed at Fredericksburg," where this Northern Plague gathered up its victims by hecatombs—"Rotting at Chancellorsville," the newly-opened Abolition Golgotha.

The plagues that afflicted the ancients and mediævals pale before our imported pestilence. We shudder as we read of them, but they lack that one element of horror that makes ours a hissing and a reproach. They were not, as ours, self-imposed and self-inflicted; they were the ministers of God's wrath, not of man's vengeance; they were angels of death, not demons of suicide; and if a determination to be rid of their plagues could have saved these people, would they have suffered? It sounds like folly to ask the question. Could our plague exist a day if we decreed its death? Not an hour, not a moment. Then, was there ever wickedness or folly like to ours? Future ages will shudder as they read of the fearful ravages committed by this Northern Plague; but will they sympathize? Will one sigh of regret escape them for the extinction of a people so unequal to their destiny?

If, like ordinary plagues, it carried off only those in whose veins the venom of its own poison lurked, then the bane would have an antidote. But unhappily for us, and unhappily for the future, whose interests we had in keeping, a mighty charge, committed to us by Time and Destiny, its course in this particular is unlike any of its physical congeners. Cunning as well as fierce, Abolitionism, by aid of an auxiliary plague, sweeps off thousands and tens of thousands who would never have succumbed to its deadly influence. Minds too healthy, souls too strong to be infected by it, are carried off by the war fever that follows in its train, and the country is cheated out of compensation. If every one tainted with Abolitionism were swept away by it, and the moral and political atmosphere purified by the carrying off of all infected bodies, then indeed the outbursts of this plague might have worked for the nation's weal. Then indeed it would have been but a blessing in disguise. But unfortunately, let this war end when it will, or how it will, it will leave the Abolitionists as strong numerically as it found them; for, though they love the scent of blood, they love to scent it afar off. They stay at home in their easy-chairs, discharging virus through their pens, and doing all that in them lies to propagate the plague that is threatening the life of the country. Oh, that our soldiers only knew what tools they were made; that the glamour were removed from their sight, so that they could see, back of the Stars and Stripes, the yellow flag of pestilence—the present battle-flag of the United States; the flag that waved at Fredericksburg and Chancellorsville; the flag that will lead them yet to heavier losses and to deeper disgrace. When that day of great awakening comes, the army of the United States will muster itself out of service.

THE LETTER OF GOVERNOR SEYMOUR.

(*From the* METROPOLITAN RECORD, *May* 30, 1863.)

IN last week's RECORD we published the manly, the spirit-stirring letter of the Governor of the State of New York, Horatio Seymour. It had in it the ring of the true metal, and its tones awakened in the heart of the people a sympathy with the feelings which dictated it, that the authorities at Washington must not, and can not, ignore without injury to their own personal and political interests.

Scorning the language of diplomacy and political intrigue, it gave expression to the sentiments of its author in the bold and manly utterances of an American freeman. There is not a man whose heart beats with the impulses of freedom that did not feel it bound with joy as he read the letter in which our State Executive denounces the arrest of Vallandigham as "an act which has brought dishonor upon our country, which is full of danger to our persons and our homes, and which bears upon its front a conscious violation of law and justice."

This is the true language in which to characterize the atrocious, the infamous proceedings of the Administration and its tools in the arrest of Hon. Clement L. Vallandigham. There is no temporizing in this, no resort to those mean subterfuges known among politicians as political expediency. That lettergives unrestrained expression to the true feelings of his heart, and they show that he has been chafing under the restraints which a long-abused patience, prudence, and forbearance imposed upon him. His letter is not only the severest rebuke which the Administration has yet received, but it is a scathing, withering denunciation of the vile nature of the proceedings by which the citizen of a free State is dragged from his home at the dead hour of night by armed men, subjected to a trial by court-martial, and secretly conveyed beyond the boundaries of a sovereign State to be incarcerated in a Government bastile.

Well might our noble and true-hearted Governor stigmatize the transaction as involving a series of offenses against our most sacred rights, as an interference with the freedom of speech, as a violation of the security of our homes, and as a mockery of justice. He does not mince his language, and the whole spirit of his letter is a simple expression of the indignation which he feels as an American citizen at the outrages that have been perpetrated on the sacred cause of liberty. Nay, he goes still further, and asserts that if this action of the authorities at Washington is sanctioned by the people, it is an act of revolution—it is the establishment of a military despotism. Whatever apprehensions might have been entertained with regard to the position of Governor Seymour, there certainly can be no doubt now, after this declaration of his principles, as to the views he entertains in reference to the policy of the Administration. It is clear that since the crowning act of its career—the arrest, military trial, and imprisonment of Mr. Vallandigham—he looks upon it as a military despotism. He naturally feels apprehensive of the liberties of the people of the great State of New York. He knows that he is the custodian of those liberties, and that he is bound by his oath of office to maintain them with all the powers and resources of the Empire State. And why is it, let us ask, that we citizens of New York are not subject to the same arbitrary despotism of which Mr. Vallandigham has been made the victim? The answer is to be found in the fact that Ohio is under a Governor who is but a creature of the Administration, while we have elected as our State Executive a man who loves liberty, and who is determined to stand by the rights of the people of the great State with the defense of whose freedom and interests he has been intrusted.

We must confess that previous to Governor Seymour's letter we had entertained some doubt as to the course he intended to pursue. But that letter, manly, bold, and outspoken as it is, has set at rest whatever misgivings we might have felt in regard to his policy. But it is not alone in his letter that we find the guarantees of his future action, for we have received assurances from those who have enjoyed the opportunity of personal intercourse with him, that he will at all hazards oppose the usurpation of the Federal Administration within the limits of the Empire

State, and meet their unconstitutional and despotic course with its whole military power and resources, if necessary.

We have, therefore, every confidence not only in the sincerity but in the resolution and *backbone* of our Governor, and we entertain no doubt whatever of the people standing by him in maintaining the sovereignty of the State. We are aware that there are a few timid and wavering people who shrink from the very contemplation of an armed collision between the State and Federal Governments; but they ought to know that it is only by th resolution and firmness of our State Executive that such a collision can be avoided. They dread, forsooth, the bombardment of the city of New York by the forts in our harbor; but the resort to so desperate an extremity would be the death-knell of the Administration, and would seal the fate of the miserable creatures of whom it is composed. We can hardly conceive the possibility of such an occurrence, of such a mad, such an insane, such a suicidal act. The bombardment of New York would be the signal of an uprising compared with which that evoked by the assault on Fort Sumter would be mere child's play. No, no; there need be no apprehension of such an act of desperation on the part of the Federal authorities. The first duty of every citizen of New York is to stand by the authority that gives protection to life and property; the authority that punishes the burglar and the murderer, *that guards the people alike against the terrors of mob violence and the usurpations of despotic power.* It is the State government from which we obtain charters for our institutions, charitable, religious, and educational. It is to the State government that we look for the redress of our grievances; it is to the State government that we must apply for the rectification of any legislative wrong; it is the State government that not only grants charters but that makes appropriations for enterprises of benevolence and charity; and it is the State government that is now establishing in this city and elsewhere houses of rest for our wounded and disabled volunteers, who have been flung aside by the Federal Administration. It is the State government that is nearest to us; it is with that we have most to do. Its courts are the most numerous; its officers are more familiar to us ; it is for its support that we are taxed, while the Federal Government is comparatively unknown to our fellow-citizens. Said Alexander Hamilton, when speaking on this subject:

"THE STATE ESTABLISHMENTS OF CIVIL AND MILITARY OFFICERS OF EVERY DESCRIPTION INFINITELY SURPASSING IN NUMBER ANY CORRESPONDING ESTABLISHMENT OF OFFICERS IN THE GENERAL GOVERNMENT WILL CREATE SUCH AN EXTENT AND COMPLICATION OF ATTACHMENTS AS WILL SECURE THE SUPPORT AND PREDILECTION OF THE PEOPLE. WHENEVER, THEREFORE, CONGRESS SHALL MEDITATE ANY INFRINGEMENTS OF THE STATE CONSTITUTIONS, THE GREAT BODY OF THE PEOPLE WILL NATURALLY TAKE PART WITH THEIR DOMESTIC REPRESENTATIVES. CAN THE GENERAL GOVERNMENT WITHSTAND SUCH A UNITED OPPOSITION? WILL THE PEOPLE SUFFER THEMSELVES TO BE STRIPPED OF THEIR PRIVILEGES? WILL THEY SUFFER THEIR LEGISLATURES TO BE REDUCED TO A SHADOW AND A NAME? THE IDEA IS SHOCKING TO COMMON SENSE."

Yet this very idea has been realized in the State of Ohio, and would be in the State of New York were it under a Republican Governor. We are, however, particularly fortunate in having a State Executive who fully understands the vital importance of his position at the present juncture, and who possesses both the courage and the firmness to meet the impending crisis.

Governor Seymour knows full well that the Administration is determined not to abandon the almost absolute power of which it is now in possession without a desperate struggle. Its assaults upon the well-defined constitutional rights of the people and upon State sovereignty afford sufficient evidence of its designs in that direction. The shallow pretext that the suspension of our rights as citizens is necessary for the overthrow of the Southern Confederacy could never deceive any man except him who has abandoned his reason and common sense to official keeping. The people of New York can not be misled by those specious devices, and they are, we feel convinced, determined to stand by our Governor at every hazard.

We are no alarmists, but we regard the infamous outrage perpetrated by the authorities at Washington upon the State sovereignty of Ohio as the most fatal blow that has yet been aimed at popular freedom. We believe it is high time to take immediate measures to put our State in a position in which she will be able to defend herself against similar encroachments by the Federal authorities. We earnestly trust that there will be no delay in this matter, and that the Governor will place *at least one hundred thousand of our militia upon a war footing.* If there are not arms enough within the limits of the State, then let them be purchased at once, and sufficient stores of ammunition accumulated. We entreat the Governor, in the name of law and order, to see to it that there be no unnecessary delay in this matter, to see to it that the people are not forced to band themselves together in independent and illegal organizations; that our lives and our properties may not be left at the mercy of armed mobs, that whatever opposition shall be made by the people against a Federal usurpation of their rights may be made under the sanction and with the authority of the State Government.

The Administration has done all in its power to foster and encourage the organization within the limits of the Empire State of societies which are pledged to the support of its unconstitutional measures, yet the men who compose these societies, these so-called "Loyal Leagues," look to the State authorities for protection to life and property, thereby acknowledging the fact that they owe the highest allegiance to the State.

If their policy prevailed, State boundaries would be broken down, and the principle of State sovereignty would be lost in a centralized despotism. We contend that such bodies are inimical to our State Government, bound as they are to the support of the policy of the Administration, whether just or unjust, constitutional or unconstitutional.

We repeat that there should be no delay, and if we may seem to be too urgent, it is from a sincere desire that the honor of the great State of which we are a citizen may not be injured and its interests may not be placed in danger by the ill-judged or irregular proceedings of men whether opposing the tyrannical acts of the Federal Administration or sustaining them under the title of Loyal Leaguers.

A POLAND IN THE UNITED STATES.

(*From the* METROPOLITAN RECORD, *May* 30, 1863.)

THIS week we have fearful intelligence from the West. A star has fallen from our Northern sky. Ohio, the Sicily of America, has been blotted out of the list of Sovereign States; her territory violated, her citizens outraged, her supremacy defied by an individual bearing the military commission of the United States. But yesterday she sat a queen, holding as high a rank in our system of confederated sovereignties as the Empire State; to-day she is a dependency of Washington, unable to assert her own sovereignty or the liberty of her citizens, unable to preserve her soil from desecration or to avenge it. Discrowned Ohio, our noble sister State, how bitterly we feel the humiliation that has fallen upon thee! And to make it the more galling, inflicted by a fugitive from Fredericksburg; a man who had neither prudence enough to keep his army out of danger nor daring enough to carry them through it. Yet this man, once out of sight of a Southern foe, becomes foolhardy, and boldly strikes at the authority of a sovereign State. He can not beat Southern soldiers, but he can browbeat Northern citizens; he can not cope with rebels, but then he is an overmatch for any loyal man in his department. Smarting from the drubbing he had received in Virginia, Burnside hastened to the West, determined to retrieve himself, and, by reducing Ohio to a state of vassalage, make amends for his misadventures in the Old Dominion. And to our sorrow, and to her shame, he has done it.

In the dead of the night his armed myrmidons swept the State, and, without the shadow of law, forced their way into a private dwelling, dragged a distinguished citizen of Ohio from his home and family, carried him beyond the boundaries of the State, beyond the protection of the legal tribunals, and delivered him over to the tender mercies of a court-martial. For what crime? For differing with the men in power on the best means of restoring the Union; for refusing to receive his political creed from Washington, and for preaching the faith that was in him "in season and out of season;" for endeavoring to instill into the people his own apprehensions, and to animate them with his own resolve; for bearing himself, in fact, as a freeman in a free State, and not as a *suspet* in a Military Department. Can American citizens of any party or politics read that episode of wrong and violence without a blush—picture to themselves the terror of the trembling household awakened in the "dead waste and middle of the night" by armed marauders—the agony of the heart-stricken, frantic wife as she saw her husband borne away, and remembered that but a few weeks previous the editor of an anti-Government paper was seized upon in the same manner and *murdered*—without shuddering sympathy?

Is it a page of English history we are reading? Is it an incident of a Cossack raid in Poland that sets our blood a-bounding? No; our sympathies are wanted nearer home. We have none to spare now for Poland or Ireland, for Posen or Hungary. We have found our Poland in the West, so sorely oppressed, so terribly beset, that it claims all our thoughts and needs all our assistance. What is Ohio, stripped of sovereignty, independence, and liberty, lorded over by a military viceroy, who holds the life, liberty, and property of its citizens in his hands, but the Poland of America? The Governor of Ohio is a thing for men to laugh at. He has seen his State degraded, his office ignored, his constituents outraged, the laws of the State contemptuously nullified by a Government that has taken up arms to put down nullification in the South; and yet he has made no sign, uttered no protest, taken no measures to obtain satisfaction for the gross insult. Would that it had happened in New York. If it had, we venture to predict that the men at Washington would have been taught a lesson that even they, obtuse as they are, would have understood. If Ohio had understood the animus of the men in Washington as well as New York does, if she rested on her arms, as every State should do at the present crisis, she would not now be mourning her lost sovereignty, and her exiled son, the gallant champion and confessor of liberty. Did she think that the liberticide, like the haughty Florentines of old, would scorn to pounce upon a foe without warning? Did she expect that such a remnant of chivalry existed in the breasts of the Lincolnites, the party that has produced Butler and Schenck, and Hooker and Hascall? Ah! there was her mistake. She forgot that "eternal vigilance is the price of liberty," and she has fallen.

Yes, we are catching up to Europe fast, and in the science of government nearing day by day her imperial models. The plant that in Europe took centuries to ripen, here, thanks to our warmer climate, is perfected in a day. Tyranny which there has been fostered by time and developed by circumstances, has here sprung up like a weed. But European tyranny is a century plant—American tyranny a mere mushroom—not a growth, but an excrescence, without a root in the soil or a branch in the air, owing its existence to accident, and deprived by nature of the means of perpetuating itself. And herein are our grounds for hope, this is our guarantee—that, though American tyranny may equal Russian in excess, it never can in duration. No! struggle as it may, it can never fasten itself upon the country; the generation that saw it rise will see it wither, and the men who, in their mad folly, allowed themselves to be used as instruments in sowing the seeds, before two years are about will regret it in bitterness of heart.

THE FUTURE.

(*From the* Metropolitan Record, *June* 6, 1863.)

It requires no prophetic vision to foresee the result of the present war. That it will terminate in the complete independence of the Southern Confederacy there can, we think, be no doubt in the mind of any rational man. We have nothing but contempt for the opinions of a party or leader who insists that the Union can be restored by the prolongation of hostilities. It is the worst kind of hypocrisy to deceive the people by holding out hopes that can never be realized, and of this hypocrisy the North has been made the deluded victim. Some of these leaders may have really believed that the South could be forced into the Union, but the majority never labored under such a delusion. A few were afraid to take any other course; a few were bribed to join the Loyal Leaguers; but the great mass imagined that there was no other way to popularity except by favoring "a vigorous prosecution of the war." In fact, the war fever swept over the North, infecting the great body of the people, leaders and all, with the exception of a few, who, like the still, small voice of conscience, were heard amid the universal din and clangor of arms. Among these the RECORD was proud to rank itself, satisfied that the time would come when its course would be justified, and the policy which it consistently advocated would prevail. Its Editor was opposed to the war from the start; he was accused of being a secessionist; he was charged with treason, and threatened with the fate which has already befallen so many of the advocates of peace. It is almost needless to state that we stand now where we have always stood; that we have nothing to retract; and that we would prefer at any time to see the Union divided into two Confederacies rather than live in a Union one portion of which would be held in military subjection to the other. Some of our friends have differed with us on this point; but the time will come—and it is fast hastening—when they will be obliged to stand upon our platform. We insisted that war could never restore the Union—that it was a Union of free-will, and not of force—that there was nothing in the Constitution or the writings of the fathers of the Revolution to justify or authorize coercion.

This, however, is of the past, and we trust its stern and terrible lessons have had their due effect upon the people of the North. They certainly should be satisfied by this time of the imbecility and the incompetency of those who compose the Administration. They have seen enough to satisfy them that the men in Washington are utterly unable to cope with the crisis, and that they will, by their policy, eventually drive the Northern States to resolve themselves into their original sovereignties. It is useless—nay, it is worse than useless—it is criminal, at this critical juncture, to deceive the people by holding out hopes that can never be realized. They have already had enough of broken promises and violated pledges, and it is now the duty of every man whose opinions are supposed to have any weight or influence in the community, to express those opinions frankly and fearlessly.

The Administration having utterly failed to subjugate the South, and the South having maintained itself gallantly and successfully against an overwhelming invasion from the North, repeated again and again, it now depends upon the States whether they shall continue to sustain the war policy, and, by so doing, establish a permanent despotism that shall sweep away the last vestiges of popular liberty from the Northern States. We do not believe that they are prepared for such a disastrous, such a fatal result, and we have therefore a few serious reflections to present in regard to the future prospects of the northern portion of the old Union, and these reflections we shall present under separate heads.

I. A Convention of the Northern States must be held to take into consideration the new condition in which they are now placed, and to devise means for their reorganization or re-confederation under a new Constitution. This Convention, if held, will be composed of delegates from each State, whose basis of representation will be fixed, not by States, but by the proportion of population. Each State, however, being sovereign, will have the power to ratify or reject the Constitution proposed and adopted in the Convention. In this respect their action will not differ from that of the States that adopted the old Constitution and formed the Union, which has been overthrown by an Abolition Administration. In that Convention, we have no doubt, the sovereignty of the States will be guarded with the same jealous care that marked their action in the Convention to which the present Constitution owes its origin.

II. The vast debt which has been accumulated by the present mad, fanatical, and suicidal war, will, as a matter of imperative necessity, be repudiated. In stating this fact, we do not seek to justify the principle of repudiation, which is alike dishonorable in a nation or an individual. We speak of such a policy now as among the inevitable consequences of the lamentable condition in which the North finds itself after an Abolition crusade of over two years. The debt of the North may now be estimated at about two thousand five hundred millions of dollars, and the interest on this, at seven per cent., would be about one hundred and eighty millions, which is larger than the interest on the national debt of England. When it is remembered that the English national debt was the growth of centuries, while ours has been created by a two-years' war, the restiveness and impatience of the American people under such a load will be fully understood and appreciated. *We do not believe they will stand it, and we entertain no doubt whatever that they will seek relief in repudiation.*

III. The people having had, through the policy of the present Administration, a pretty fair experience of a military despotism, will instruct their delegates to the aforesaid Convention to insist upon the inviolability of State rights, the sovereignty of the States, the liberty of the press, the freedom of speech, habeas corpus, and all the rights guaranteed by the present Constitution. Upon these important points they will be so explicit and so direct as to leave no possible grounds for apprehension in the future.

IV. Admitting the existence of two Confederacies within the limits of the old Union, the Government established under the new Constitution will have to deal with the important question of boundaries, customs, river navigation, and the general relations that may spring up between the two Confederacies. It is essential that these relations should not be complicated; that they should, in fact, be so simple and so easily understood as to avoid the possibility of future collisions. We trust that there will be entire free trade between the two Republics, so as to render border custom-houses entirely unnecessary. The navigation of the Mississippi will, and must be, free to the Gulf of Mexico; any other arrangement will be inevitably productive of future wars.

V. As friendly relations between the two Confederacies are essential to the welfare and the future prosperity of both, it should be the policy of the Northern, as we trust it will be of the Southern, to discourage and frown down every attempt to create hostile or bitter feelings between their respective governments and peoples. As for the North, its commercial and profit-seeking people will be among the first in the effort to obliterate the past, and to sink its unpleasant memories in the gulf of oblivion. It must be acknowledged that the Northern people are, to a great extent, like the English, "a nation of shopkeepers," and that *the present war has been waged as much to retain the custom of the South as to maintain the Union.* Now, we venture to say that none will be more anxious or more earnest to exhibit their friendly feelings toward the people of the South than the very men who have been, and are still, so rampant for a vigorous prosecution of the war; nay, we not only believe this, but we believe also that they will be the greatest toadies of the South; that they will be profuse in their professions of good-will and friendly feeling; that they will *fete* and toast "our Southern brethren" at the future banquets that will be given to them in Northern cities; that they will never tire in speaking or writing of a common origin, a common ancestry, a common language, and all those other things which we have been accustomed to hear at convivial assemblies of Americans and Englishmen. All this we shall, most probably, see within a very few years in this our own day and generation.

VI. We have referred to the Convention of the Northern States as among the inevitable consequences of this war and the condition to which the North has been reduced. It is possible, but we do not regard it as probable, that the North shall witness another Presidential election before that Convention shall have taken place. This is a melancholy reflection, but we are considering our present position, and dealing with the hard substantial facts that have been forced upon our consideration. If we could blot out the memories, the sad, bitter recollections of the past two years and a half, oh! how willingly would we do so. It is not we, or such as we, who have destroyed this Union. The murderers of this nation, the assassins of the Republic, are to be found in Washington in the members of the present Administration, who, with their co-conspirators, the Abolitionists, have overthrown the Union, and are now seeking to bury in the same grave with it the vestiges of American freedom. Taking it for granted that the Administration has not only destroyed the Republic, but that by its manner of prosecuting the war, its confiscation and emancipation measures, its vandalism in the destruction of Southern cities and Southern homes, its war upon the freemen of the North, upon State sovereignty, as well as its nullification of all the guarantees of the Constitution—taking it for granted that the Administration has by such instrumentalities not only destroyed the Republic, but is now seeking to permanently fasten a military despotism upon the North, the free States will be compelled, in their own defense, and for the preservation of their independence, to begin anew the process of re-construction and re-formation. The men who have not been committed to the Abolition policy of the Government must be selected for the performance of this work. *Abolitionism must be abolished* if we would preserve friendly relations with the South with the view to an offensive and defensive alliance of the two great Republics of America against the intrigues and machinations of foreign powers.

VII. It is possible that the memories of wrongs and outrages committed during a ruthless invasion of the South may render such an alliance a work of difficulty for many years; but the statesmen of the South will, we believe, be the first to perceive the necessity for, and the benefits derivable from, such relationship between the two Republics. It would be as much their interest as ours to establish and preserve these relations between the North and the South. Such an arrangement would do away with the necessity of large standing armies and expensive navies. If we mistake not there is a treaty between the United States and Great Britain in regard to the great lakes, by which the maintenance of a large naval force in those waters is rendered unnecessary. As for the settlement of Abolitionism, there will, we think, be less trouble than when the South was in the Union. We may not have a Fugitive Slave Law, and we may; but whether we shall have or shall not have one, we think the great majority of the people of the North have sufficiently shown that they are not desirous of a further increase in the negro population of these States. They are excluded from Illinois by legislative enactment, and in other States such demonstrations have been made against the introduction of contrabands as ought to satisfy any rational mind that they are not considered desirable additions to the population. In fact, Mr. Lincoln himself may be quoted in proof of the reliability and truth of these statements. His interview with the colored delegation that visited him about a year ago, in which he told them that they could not live as freemen in the same community with the whites without injury to the latter, is pretty satisfactory on this point, as is also his effort to colonize them in Central America, whether that effort shall prove a failure or a success.

VIII. One of the most difficult questions to settle will be that of the Territories, which, if not settled definitely and conclusively by a convention between the two Confederacies, may lead to endless disputes, and perhaps hostilities. It may be that the old Missouri Compromise line will be adopted; but, whatever line may be adopted as the limit of the Northern and Southern territories, that line must be clearly and distinctly drawn. Whatever disputes may arise about these Territories, they certainly can not originate in any fear that either Confederacy will not have sufficient land to meet the demands of their population for two or three centuries to come. In fact, the growth of population on this continent, although unprecedentedly rapid, will not be adequate for generations to the settlement and the cultivation of the almost illimitable domain that stretches west of the Mississippi away to the Rocky Mountains.

IX. At the close of the war, a new question will come up for the consideration of that portion that still remains of the old Union. This is no less a question than the future position of the border slave States. If the principle of universal suffrage is to prevail with regard to the election of their choice between the North and the South, then that question must be left to their own decision by a general election in each State, and with regard to the selection, we believe that if left entirely untrammeled by governmental or bayonet interference, they will decide by large majorities of their populations to go with the Southern Confederacy. There is one substantial reason for arriving at this conclusion. These States are bound together by common sympathies, by common interests, and by the institution of slavery, which is common to all. These are like so many links of steel; but, independent of these considerations, the fact that all of them, with one exception, have been made the theater of war, and have been subjected to the full force of the Washington tyranny and its military satraps, affords of itself sufficient grounds for the belief that they will go with the South. It is absurd to urge in refutation of this position that, if they conclude to remain with the Northern States, their slaves will not be interfered with. What power on earth can guarantee this in view of the rampant, despotic Abolitionism that has taken possession even of the Government itself? What guarantee have they, even, that in the event of interference with the peculiar institution, they will be compensated by Government for the emancipation of their slaves? In this connection, let us ask, what has become of the offer to purchase the freedom of the slaves in Kentucky and Missouri? Do we not all know that the proposed manumission, so far as Missouri and Kentucky are concerned, has turned out to be a miserable failure? Of the whole two thousand five hundred millions of dollars expended during the war, we doubt if one million was appropriated to purchase the freedom of slaves. Such is the result of a sentiment that has convulsed the country throughout its entire extent; that has led to the sacrifice of some six or seven hundred thousand lives; that has made the land to resound with the wails of the widows and the orphans; and that has overthrown the mightiest Republic the world has ever seen. Who believes that, with the full knowledge of all these facts, the border slave States would be willing to remain with the North if they are afforded an opportunity of linking their destiny with that of the South?

We have endeavored, calmly and dispassionately, to discuss the condition to which the country is fast hastening, and in doing so we have been governed solely by a frank and candid desire to consider the various issues which must inevitably grow out of that condition. We feel, we believe, that not a few of our readers will differ with us in the conclusions at which we have arrived, that they still cling to the hope of a restored Union, and that the time will come when the States shall resume their old relations toward each other. We respect their feelings, and we know they will believe us when we say that no sacrifice would be too great for us to make to restore the Republic to its former unity, prosperity, and position among the nations of the earth. But the policy of the Administration has rendered this impossible, *and we have now to deal with accomplished facts.* We shall ask our readers, one and all, even those who differ with us, to take a brief review of the past, and from the light which it affords to draw their own conclusions with regard to the future. If they should coincide in our views, we shall be satisfied that the arguments we have presented are not without some weight and influence, while we do not wish to dissipate any well-founded hopes that may exist with regard to the attainment of an end so much desired by us all. Let us, then, without further preface, take a glance at the events of the past two years, and the present condition of the country.

When Mr. Lincoln was inaugurated he took a most solemn oath to fulfill his constitutional obligations, and he subsequently pledged himself not to interfere with the peculiar institution in the slave States.

Let us see how far his actions have accorded with his promises. With the most indecent haste slavery was abolished in the District of Columbia, the signature of the President giving his sanction to the law. A measure was set on foot for emancipation in the border States to which Mr. Lincoln gave his influence; but the Abolition policy of his Administration was developed most prominently and most insidiously in the Confiscation and Emancipation acts, which were almost exclusively aimed at the peculiar institution. In these various instances the most conclusive proof was afforded to the South that the whole strength and power of the Government was enlisted in a grand Abolition crusade.

The Union men of that section of the Republic were now satisfied that they had nothing to hope for, and were forced, however unwillingly, into the ranks of the secessionists. The South, by this policy, was consolidated into one compact mass, to destroy which all the power of the North has been launched against it again and again without success. But there was another feature which became, as time wore on, more and more apparent. This was the imbecility, the utter incompetency of the Administration to cope with the crisis; and this feature is now acknowledged by its erstwhile warmest supporters. It has had over two thousand millions of dollars and nearly a million and a half of men with which to subjugate the South; for, after all, it must be admitted that this is a war of subjugation. Well, this war of subjugation is a total failure, as Douglas, and Clay, and Webster, and Hamilton, and Madison, and other great statesmen of the country predicted. What have we accomplished by it? The complete alienation of the Southern States, with their seven or eight millions of American freemen. We have had, it is true, some refugees from the Southern States, who have endeavored to create such a sympathy as should manifest itself in the substantial character of pecuniary support. These men have told us wonderful stories of a Union feeling south of Mason and Dixon's line. But what has that Union feeling accomplished? Absolutely nothing.

Battle after battle has been fought, the Union army being oftener vanquished than victorious; and it is now confessed that the Southern Confederacy was never so defiant, so powerful, or so able in every way to maintain its independence as it is at the present time. It is doubtful if the effective force of the Union army exceeds five hundred thousand men—indeed, we are of the opinion that it is not much over four hundred thousand.

Is any one mad enough to imagine that such a force is equal to the overthrow of the armies commanded by Lee, and Johnston, and Bragg, and Beauregard, and the other great generals of the South? Is any man so insane as to believe that McClellan, even had he the genius of Napoleon himself, would be equal to such a task? What a delusion, then, to flatter ourselves with the hope that a people *who know their strength, and who have tested it through the ordeal of a two-years' war, the most sanguinary, the most disastrous, the most expensive on record*, will be inclined to give up that independence for which they have fought so long, struggled so valiantly, and sacrificed so much?

But then again we are told that the resources of the North in men and money are equal to a continuance of the war for two years more, and longer if need be, while some, in the height of their folly, in the excess of their absurdity, tell us that they will fight until the last man and the last dollar in the treasury is expended. Such talk is unworthy of a moment's consideration. Let us tell those who indulge in this bombastic nonsense that the conscription is already a failure; that a hundred thousand men can not be raised by it; that there are hardly enough hands left to perform the manual labor of the country; that Massachusetts, with all her efforts to recruit, even among the black population, is twenty thousand behind her quota; that the military arrests of Burnside and Hascall in the West have roused a feeling of indignation which may at any time burst forth in all the horrors of civil strife; that the confidence of the people in the Administration, its generals, and the final success of this war, is gone, utterly gone; and that the great mass of our people are sick and tired of this fruitless waste of blood and treasure.

Is not this the true state of the case? What hypocrisy, then, to talk of a further prolongation of hostilities! Let us not be deceived any longer by temporizing, by insincere and tricky politicians. Let us rise up manfully and meet the issues that have been forced upon us by those assassins of the Republic who have so long played the part which history tells us was played by Nero while gazing on the burning ruins of the Eternal City. Let us accept the "logic of accomplished facts," and manfully and courageously resolve that although the Union has been destroyed, our liberties shall still be preserved, and democratic freedom saved from the wreck of our once proud, free, and happy Republic. Let us perform the task that remains to us, and leave to time the work of reuniting in the bonds of a powerful alliance the now severed sections of a once grand confederacy.

WHICH IS THE MOST HUMILIATING—PEACE OR WAR?

(*From the* METROPOLITAN RECORD, *June* 13, 1863.)

AFTER more than two years of a fratricidal war there are some in the North who are still not only in favor of its vigorous prosecution, but who denounce as traitors and secessionists all those who are bold enough to advocate peace as the only means left of preserving the Northern States from the horrors of a fixed military despotism. These men insist that the war shall still go on, that tens, and, if need be, hundreds of thousands shall be added to the holocaust already offered up at the shrine of Abolitionism; that the press must be silenced; that liberty of speech must be suppressed; that all our constitutional guarantees must be held in abeyance until the South is thoroughly subdued. They are the last-dollar-in-the-treasury men, the firm supporters of the Administration, the advocates of a strong government, who allow no one to be right but themselves, and who insist that peace upon any other terms than the complete submission of the South would be humiliating and degrading to the North. They presume to have the honor of the country in their keeping, and from their judgment there must be no appeal.

Now, does any one imagine that these men are willing of themselves to make any sacrifices in support of their own policy? Who are they that talk to us in this dictatorial, domineering style? They are the officials of the Government, the shoddy contractors, the men who are making their profits out of all this lavish expenditure of blood and money. They are in favor of the war policy, because it adds to their ill-gotten gains. It is they who threaten the advocates of peace with all the terrors of the Washington tyranny. It is they, and such as they, who talk of the disgrace and humiliation of entering into negotiations with "rebels in arms." But what greater humiliation and disgrace could befall a country than to be governed by such a set of imbeciles, such traitors to the Constitution, as the men in Washington? What could be more humiliating to a free people than the deprivation of their rights, than the occurrence of such acts as have been committed in the West by the military satraps, Burnside and Hascall? What could be more degrading than the position in which we have been placed before the world by the wretched minions and tools of a would-be irresponsible despotism? Are we so desirous of still greater humiliations than those which have befallen us? If we are, then let the war go on, let the conscription be carried into operation without opposition. Let our brave and unjustly treated volunteers be slaughtered by tens of thousands, and their families starve at home for want of the pay to which they are fairly entitled, but which is withheld that contractors may not be kept waiting; let the citizens' last weapon against tyranny—the vote by ballot—be overthrown by the bayonet. Let all this be done if we are in favor of a prolongation of hostilities, but let us not be told that any peace could be more humiliating than a war carried on at such a fearful sacrifice to human liberty and the rights of American citizenship.

Humiliating! Look at the national capital; look at the intrigues that are going on there against the sovereignty of the States, and against the perpetuity of free institutions! Read of the doings of the wretched cabal, and do not wonder that such men as Hooker and Burnside, and Hunter and Halleck are allowed to play their pranks before high Heaven. Look and estimate if you can the character of the man who can tell his ribald jests while the country is bleeding at every pore. Look there and wonder not that the humiliation of the country should be the subject of a boast with his Secretary of State, who, claiming to be a freeman among freemen, coolly informed a foreign minister that by merely touching the bell at his right hand he could order the arrest of any citizen of the North. *Could he do that with a citizen of the South? No! for the dominions of the military despotism at Washington do not extend within the lines of the Confederate forces.*

This war must cease if we do not desire a still greater humiliation; this war must cease if we would preserve our free institutions; this war must cease if we would not be ground down to the earth by the burdens of an excessive taxation; and, finally, this war must cease if we would avoid civil strife and anarchy in our Northern States.

AND IT WILL CEASE FROM SHEER NECESSITY.

The people have at last become aroused to a true sense of their danger. They now fully understand the character of the men who have driven the ship of state among the breakers. Their patience is exhausted, their forbearance gone, their confidence undermined, and their suspicions at last fully and actively aroused. Upon whom, then, is the Government to rely for the means wherewith to continue this war? Is it on the men who exclaim against peace as *humiliating*? Is it on the Abolitionists, under the lead of such men as Lloyd Garrison and Wendell Phillips, and Beecher and Cheever? Is it, in a word, on the contractors and tax collectors, and Government officials generally, who are so sensitive with regard to the honor of the country? No, no; these are not the men who are ready to put themselves in jeopardy, so long as they can purchase exemption from the draft by the payment of three hundred dollars worth of greenbacks. We appeal to you, mechanics and laborers, whose families are dependent upon your honest toil for support, if you are willing to sacrifice yourselves for the further enslavement of the white man, and the emancipation of a race whom President Lincoln has told you could not exist in the same community without injury to yourselves. Those anti-peace men talk to you of humiliation, while tens, ay hundreds, of thousands have been reduced by the loss of their protectors, to the bitter humiliation of destitution and poverty. What sacrifices have they made that they should oppose the re-establishment of peace? Ah! rather ask *how much would they lose by the discontinuance of this war?*

Yes, this war must cease for want of the means to carry it on. The Conscription is already a failure, and any attempt to enforce it in the North may precipitate a revolution, in which the Administration will inevitably go down. There are at the present time hardly four hundred thousand effective men in the field; the South is still invincible, still defiant; Hooker still leads the Army of the Potomac;

Burnside commands in the West, and Halleck and Stanton still rule the War Department; while over all presides the jocular and mirth-provoking Executive, with a new joke for every defeat, and a flow of *animal* spirits that no reverses or calamity can subdue. Who, then, talks of a further prolongation of the war? Are men to be stamped out of the earth? Will the citizens of the North submit to be driven like sheep to the shambles? Although the people have thus far submitted to great humiliation, we do not believe that they are prepared to yield their birthrights without a desperate struggle.

If the Conscription is attempted to be enforced, the flames of a civil war will be enkindled within the Northern States. The Administration may think that it will be easy to suppress a popular uprising by the aid of the army; but we tell them if they rely upon the army for the enslavement of their fellow-citizens, they will find that they are leaning upon a broken reed. The army are of the people and with the people, and the brave fellows who compose it can not be converted into the tools of the despots at Washington. The ties of kindred, the home affections that twine around their hearts, the associations of their youth and of their manhood, all these bind them to the respective States of which they are citizens, and any attempt of the Administration to divorce them from these sacred and powerful influences will fail—utterly, wholly, ignominiously fail. The Washington authorities have indeed been reduced to desperate straits, and we believe that a general feeling of trepidation and alarm prevails in the White House and its surroundings. They may, however, attempt to intimidate the people by a still further display of military force like that which took place at Indianapolis, at Newark, and at other places; but by so doing they will only expose their weakness the more, for in a contest between the States and the General Government we have the assurance of Madison and Hamilton that the States will inevitably be victorious.

Let the peace men, then, have no fears for the future. This war is near its termination. It is a fixed fact that the force in the field is entirely inadequate to its further prosecution.

Rosecrans is in want of reinforcements; Banks is in want of reinforcements; Hooker is in want of reinforcements; Grant is in want of reinforcements. The two years' and nine months' men are returning to their homes. The Administration dare not enforce the Conscription Act; huge peace meetings are being held all over the North; Massachusetts is twenty thousand behind her quota; the enormous bounties fail in inducing men to recruit; the people are becoming exceedingly uneasy under the development of the tax law; the imbecility and incompetency of the Executive and his Cabinet Council have become fixed facts in the popular mind; the action of some of the State courts, deciding that Treasury notes are not legal tenders, have shaken the confidence of the people in the value of greenbacks; and, finally, we believe that this same people are far ahead of their leaders in their desire and demand for peace.

But it is asked, how is peace to be brought about? In the first place we must have an armistice, then a convention between the Commissioners appointed to negotiate the terms of peace between the two Republics. We endeavored in last week's paper to suggest the terms upon which a permanent peace might be established; and we frankly believe that these terms form the most practical basis of settlement. To some such arrangement as this we must eventually come, even should the war be protracted for two years more.

If we are ever to have a Union again, it will, as we have already stated, and as we firmly believe, take the form of an alliance between the two Republics against the intrigues, and, it may be, the attempted domination of foreign powers in the affairs of this Continent, and such an alliance may eventually lead to a reunion on a different, but, let us trust, a stronger and more enduring basis.

THE CONSCRIPTION.

(*From the* Metropolitan Record, *June* 13, 1863.)

Is any man so foolish as to imagine that the unconstitutional act for the conscription of our fellow-citizens can really be carried into operation? Do they suppose that the people will submit to such an exaction on the very life-blood of the country? If there are such men they must be blind to the events that are daily transpiring. No, there will be no conscription, and any effort to carry such a measure into execution will prove a total failure. The Administration has lost its power, and its motion, like the diminished speed of a railroad train after it has been detached from the locomotive, is but the impetns given it by the power which it once possessed, but which is gone forever.

The people are now thoroughly wide awake; they see that they have been deceived; they know that the Administration has falsified its pledges—has attempted to steal away their liberties, and that it is fast becoming utterly powerless to wreak its wicked will by overthrowing the sovereignty of the States.

But it is barely possible that an attempt to carry out the Conscription Act may yet be made, and it is well to consider such a thing among the probabilities of the future.

In this State we believe it will be opposed by the people, and its constitutionality tested before our courts. Now, it so happens that the opinion, the indignant protest of one of the noblest Americans that ever lived, has been placed on record against the tyranny of such an imposition. We feel proud in announcing the fact that this man was a Catholic—yes, a Catholic in the truest sense of the term. His name is William Gaston, and it should be written in letters of living light wherever freedom has its worshipers. He was one of the ablest of American jurists, and his name is a synonym for judicial integrity, manly courage, heroic devotion to the truth and the right wherever that name is known. His father was murdered during the Revolution by a band of Tories, who were then engaged in an attempt somewhat similar to that of the Abolition traitors at Washington to steal away the liberties of the people. Well might Judge Gaston say, when referring to this event—

"I was baptized an American in the blood of a murdered father."

Judge Gaston was born in Newbern, North Carolina, and was elevated to the bench of the Supreme Court of that State, maintaining the highest reputation ever enjoyed by a member of the American bench. He died on the 23d of January, 1843, and the manner of his death is so remarkable that we can not forego the opportunity of referring to it here. Relating some anecdotes of his experience in Washington, he spoke of a freethinker whom he once met there. "From that day," said he, "I always looked on that man with distrust. I do not say that a freethinker may not be an honorable man, or that he may not, from high motives, scorn to do a mean act; but I dare not trust him. A belief in an all-ruling Divinity, who shapes our ends, whose eye is upon us, and who will reward us according to our deeds, is necessary. We must believe and feel that there is a God, all-wise and almighty."

These were the last words he ever uttered, for, rising to give greater emphasis to the expression, he fell back and expired.

This great man has, as we have stated, left his opinion in regard to conscription on record. The speech which he delivered in the House of Representatives in February, 1814, when referring to the great efforts made by the Administration of that day to fill up the army by conscription, one would imagine was a prophetic description of the present time:

"THE MOST ENORMOUS PRICE IS BID FOR SOLDIERS THAT WAS EVER OFFERED IN ANY AGE OR COUNTRY. SHOULD THIS FAIL, WHAT IS THE NEXT SCHEME? THERE IS NO RESERVE OR CONCEALMENT. IT HAS BEEN AVOWED THAT THE NEXT SCHEME IS A CONSCRIPTION. IT IS KNOWN THAT THIS SCHEME WAS RECOMMENDED EVEN AT THIS SESSION BY THE WAR DEPARTMENT, AND THAT IT WAS POSTPONED ONLY TO TRY FIRST THE EFFECT OF ENORMOUS BOUNTY. THE FREEMEN OF THIS COUNTRY ARE TO BE DRAFTED FROM THE RANKS OF THE MILITIA, AND FORCED ABROAD AS MILITARY MACHINES, TO WAGE A WAR OF

CONQUEST! SIR, I HAVE BEEN ACCUSTOMED TO CONSIDER THE LITTLE SHARE WHICH I HAVE IN THE CONSTITUTION OF THESE UNITED STATES AS THE MOST VALUABLE PATRIMONY I HAVE TO LEAVE TO THOSE BEINGS IN WHOM I HOPE MY NAME AND REMEMBRANCE TO BE PERPETUATED, BUT I DO SOLEMNLY DECLARE, THAT IF SUCH A DOCTRINE BE ENGRAFTED INTO THIS CONSTITUTION, I SHALL REGARD IT AS WITHOUT VALUE, AND CARE NOT FOR ITS PRESERVATION."

The language of this great and good judge is peculiarly applicable now, and contains a lesson which can not be ignored without entailing the most fearful consequences.

This is a war of invasion as that against which Judge Gaston protested, for the conscription of that day was with the view of invading Canada. It is even worse; for it is a war against the Constitution and against the writings of the fathers of the Revolution, in which there is no authority for the coercion of a sovereign State. If compromise had not been discarded, and the law of brute force had not been appealed to in the attempt to bring back the South, the restoration of the old Union would not be among the impossibilities of the future.

THE ADMINISTRATION TELEGRAPH; OR, HOW IT IS DONE.

A PLAY IN THREE ACTS.

(WRITTEN EXPRESSLY FOR THE "METROPOLITAN RECORD," AND NOT TO BE PERFORMED IN ANY THEATER, TO AVOID THE ARREST OF THE ACTORS.)

(*From the* METROPOLITAN RECORD, *June* 20, 1863.)

DRAMATIS PERSONÆ.

ABE LITION LINKEM.
W. H. HIRELAW.
SOLOMON GREENBACK.
SECRETARY BLUSTER.
SECRETARY SPRINGS.
CONFIDENTIAL CLERK OF SECRETARY HIRELAW.
GENERAL MALLET.
THE INTELLIGENT CONTRABAND.
THE RELIABLE SOUTHERN GENTLEMAN.
PORTER.

ACT I.

SCENE 1.

Secret office in the War Department.—SEC. HIRELAW *presiding over a meeting of the War Telegraph Bureau.*

SEC. HIRELAW—Well, gentlemen, did I not tell you that my plan would be the most successful? An experience of forty years in public life has satisfied me that the people are easily gulled. Did you not see how I cajoled them when at the Astor House in the great metropolis I said, and pledged my word thereto, that three short months would see the termination of this war. 'Tis true the pledge was not redeemed; but, sirs, the popular heart 's a generous one, and its trust once given is not soon withdrawn. If proof of this were needed, see how my political promissory note has been renewed, until now the time is extended to nine times three months! Am I not right, then, in my conclusions? Yes, sirs. What follows as the inevitable inference? Lie on, and they will still believe, for a lie well told must make its way. But what news to-day from Vicksburg? Has that Sebastapol not fallen yet, or is Pemberton determined to hold out? What is Grant doing, and what is he about? The agent of the Memphis telegraph should have captured it before this. Send him word at once to say the fate of Vicksburg is sealed, that our starry flag now floats upon its ramparts.

ALL—Good.

SEC. H.—If 'tis not taken, it ought, and that's the same. If not yet in Grant's possession, it should be; so we'll take it for *grant*-ed.

ABE LINKEM—Stay! hold, Mr. Secretary; not so fast, I pray you. Your joke on Grant reminds me of a capital anecdote of an old chum of mine who floated rafts down the crooked Mississippi—darn the thing! I wish it was straightened out—*anyhow, it's full of snags.* Well, this friend of mine said he'd bet drinks that his family was as old as creation—(his name was Grant, too)—so I bet him; but, by thunder! he beat me, for he showed me in the Bible where it said, "there were Grants in those days." And there, sure enough, it was, for the printer who set it up spelt it grants instead of giants, so, by thunder! he got me. [*All indulge in laughter.*

GEN. MALLET—Ha! ha! really that's very good, Mr. President. Giants and Grants! Capital! Ha! ha!

ABE L. [*aside to Gen. Mallet*]—Capital joke! "My wife says so, too." By the way, General, who did you say you wanted appointed to that brigadier-generalship?

[*The General whispers.*

He shall have it, and my word's better than a three-months' note of Secretary Hirelaw.

SEC. H.—I asked what news from Vicksburg. Why this hesitation?

INTELLIGENT CONTRABAND—It's not yet taken, and "dat's what's de matter." Massa, General Pemberton says he won't allow it noways nohow. He's got plenty grub, and says he'll fight Gen. Grant, "or any other man," as long as he has a horse or a dog left.

GEN. M.—Who said that this was an intelligent contraband? He is not the man we want. Away with him. So. Is he gone?

VOICES—He's gone.

[*Chorus in the distance.*]

"He is gone where the good darkies go."

So lay down the shovel and the hoe,
Dere are no more work for
De poor contraband,
For a sojering he must go.

GEN. M.—Where is the reliable Southern gentleman?

R. S. GENTLEMAN [*aside to Mallet*]—What about that office you promised? You know my story is dependent on that.

GEN. M. [*aside*]—You shall have it; but is the story a good one?

R. S. G. [*aside*—You shall see.] Gentlemen, I have just arrived from Richmond, and the cabinet of that arch traitor Davis is now stricken with fear at the wretched prospect before them. There is not three weeks' provisions in the whole South, the soldiers are on the verge of mutiny, the blockade is impassable, and in less than three weeks the Southern Confederacy must collapse.

SEC. H.—By Jove! Mallet, that won't do; he goes ahead of me. He says three weeks, while I have promised three months.

GEN. M.—Never mind, Bill, *you're both equally re-lie-able.*

R. S. G. [*aside to Mallet*]—What think you of my story?

GEN. M.—Truly, you have a most inventive genius, and if you have not overwhelmed them at the South, you have enabled us *to do* the North. You shall have the office promised. [*Exit R. S. Gentleman et omnes.*

SCENE 2.

A Private Chamber in the Navy Department—SEC. SPRINGS, *surnamed "The Old Man of the Sea," discovered sitting at a table surrounded by charts, plans of Monitors, etc.*

SEC. SPRINGS [*soliloquizing*]—Nine more vessels gone through that confounded Alabama. This is more than human patience can endure. The fates are all against me; and e'en the daily press can find no better subject for its comments. *I* have made no three months' promises, *I* have issued no political promissory notes. Why, then, should *I* be so baited? There's a vicious fellow must make a pun upon my name by asking if "all is well that *ends* Welles?" Springs he should have said, but it's near enough for a joke. 'Twas but last night I had a dream, and in that dream methought a whole army of these editors rushed upon me with pens upraised as if to strike me to the earth. Their banner bore these words in golden characters:

"THE PEN IS MIGHTIER THAN THE SWORD."

"'Tis false," I cried, "the pen's not mightier than the sword." The little bell of Sec. Hirelaw* has twice the power, and has it not been proved ere this that the dollar is all-mighty? I know a change is working in the public mind, and that in the President's own State the suppression policy has met with a repulse that may be but the beginning of disaster. Ha! who knocks? I trust no further news about the Alabama. Enter.

[*The door opens, and* SEC. HIRELAW *enters.*

SEC. H.—Glad to see you, old fellow. What's the news from the dominions of the saline god, that tough old salt, called Neptune?

SEC. S.—A truce to joking, Bill. You know I am thin-skinned, and can not even hear the name of Semmes without a shudder.

SEC. H.—Well, well, no joke, I assure you. Why not do as I do? Laugh at their assaults, and whene'er you get a chance, revenge yourself by sending your assailant to Fort McHenry or Lafayette. Springs, my boy, you're not up to trap. If you only knew this people as well as I do, no fears of the future would perplex your thoughts by day or dreams by night. Do you not see how easily they are cowed, and how passively they submit themselves to the yoke?

SEC. S.—That may or may not be so; but still I dread the future. The people, I grant you, have been patient,

* MR. SEWARD TO LORD LYONS—My lord, I can touch a bell on my right hand and order the arrest of a citizen in Ohio. I can touch the bell again and order the imprisonment of a citizen of New York; and no power on earth but that of the President can release them. Can the Queen of England in her dominions do as much?

not passive, and the time may come—but let's not think of that. The subject's an unpleasant one. What news from the Mississippi? is Vicksburg taken?

SEC. H.—Yes.

SEC. S.—How? by assault?

SEC. H.—No, by telegraph, and—a reliable Southern gentleman, who is to be rewarded for the feat by the sale to your department of one of his old mud-scows, and an office in mine.

SEC. S.—Now, I prithee, Bill, no more such tricks. Have I not enough of mud-scows? Must I again be tortured by the press? My mind is on the *rack* already.

SEC. H.—Pshaw! In diplomacy you are but a child.

SEC. S.—Well, well, have it so. I must confess I can not look so calmly on these things as my able colleague of the State Department. There is that affair at Charleston—

SEC. H.—I should think you had enough of Charleston already. Come, you must dine with me to-day, and as we have no time to lose, put by the cares of office for the present, and we'll have a right good jolly hour.

SEC. S.—Agreed. I am at your service. [*Exeunt.*

ACT II.

SCENE 1.

An Attic in the Negro quarter of the Capital—INTELLIGENT CONTRABAND *employed in demolishing a plate of fried eels.*

INT. CONTRABAND—By golly! dis chile was not wide awake dat time; but he has larned a lesson *dis time*, anyhow. Dey don't want de trufe. So I guess I'll have to do a little lyin. I'll just take Vicksburg right straight off, and put the banner, or the banger, on the bafflement. Guess dat'll fetch him. Ya! ya! Sure I be an intelligent contraband, and if I aint smart enuff for um dis time dis nigger knows nuffin, dat's all. I jis go right straight off and tell him Vicksburg is took.

SCENE 2.

Residence of SEC. HIRELAW—*The Sec. and his confidential Clerk engaged in earnest conversation.*

SEC. HIRELAW—Your plan's a good one. I admire it. It will not do t' oppose these peace men too strong at first. We must feel the public pulse and see how it beats. That mistake of Burnside's has thrown us back somewhat. It came too soon after Vallandigham's banishment. We must revoke the order. Your advice is a good one. And then—I think I understand you—then we must observe a little moderation, and seem to yield while we are but strengthening the chain. The conscription! Ha! Yes, the conscription must succeed, and to secure that success, concessions, apparent concessions, to the popular demands are wise and statesmanlike. But let the conscription succeed, and we are masters of the situation. Do I not understand you?

CON. CLERK—Fully; that is my idea, for if the people will submit to that, then the triumph of our scheme is certain. You, by securing the prolongation of the war, are enabled to wield the military power of the country. Six hundred thousand conscripts are sufficient for the conquest of the North, and the Emperor of France has set a lesson that may well be copied—a *coup d'état* would soon dispose of all who talk such treason as that defunct and musty document, the Constitution, contains.

SEC. H.—These are words of wisdom such as Richelieu himself could not surpass; but we must end this consultation. There are other matters of import to look after, and they can not be put aside.

CON. C.—Ah! there is one thing I had well-nigh forgot.

SEC. H.—Delay not, then, for you see I am hurried, and to-morrow must be given to *telegraph inventions and inventors.*

CON. C.—To be brief, there is a paper published in New York which is noted for its devoted advocacy of Free Speech, Free Press, and treason such as that must not be allowed.

SEC. H.—Name the paper, and it shall be attended to.

CON. C.—The METROPOLITAN RECORD. Nay, start not at the name.

SEC. H.—Ha! sayst thou so—the RECORD? Why, me-thought it was the loyalest among the loyal. It must be stopped. *Where's my bell?*

CON. C.—I know not. It has been astray betimes since that man Seymour was elected Governor of the Empire State.

SEC. H.—Well, as we can do nothing in New York without that bell, and as Seymour may interfere, we must bide our time. So farewell, my trusty friend, till we two meet again. [*Exeunt.*

ACT III.

SCENE 1.

The secret office in the War Department, as represented in Act I., Scene 1.

ABE LITION LINKEM—Are we all together?

SEC. HIRELAW—I believe the meeting is full, and so now to business. What's on the table?

ABE L.—Paper, pens, and ink, and—my two legs. Ha! ha! that's a good one. Aint it, Mallet?

GEN. MALLET—Capital. Ha! ha!

ABE L. [*aside to Mallet*]—I'll appoint your friend brig-adier-general sure. I have a capital joke to tell you when we're alone, and Hirelaw aint around.

SOLOMON GREENBACK—This, I believe, is a meeting of *telegraph inventors*, and I would therefore suggest that as government stock is running down in the market, it might be as well to get out a good startling dispatch from Vicks-burg.

GEN. M.—The very thing which brought us together. Matters, it must be confessed, look very hazy in that quar-ter at the present time. What say you, Springs?

SEC. SPRINGS—There I agree with you. 'Tis true my gun-boats and mortars have been hammering at them for weeks with poor success, but a telegraphic dispatch is the thing to use them up and put a quietus on the discon-tented North.

ALL—Then let us have the dispatch.

PORTER [*entering and addressing Secretary Hirelaw*]—The Intelligent Contraband is without, and asks to be admitted.

SEC. H.—Admit him.

[*Intelligent Contraband makes his appearance, and says:*

Massa Hirelaw, I've been tinkin' 'bout dat matter since, and, by golly! I find dat 'twas all a mistake of dis nigger. Massa Pemberton's done gone. Whew! he can't stand no time. He got only five horses for his men, and dey so tin for want ob fodder, dat dere notin' but skin and bone. Dey'll be starved right out in two or free days.

SEC. H.—How long since you were there?

INT. CON.—Ise just come from dar right straight.

SEC. H.—That's capital; that'll do. [*To his confidential clerk*]—See that he's well paid for that information.

[*Exit Int. Contraband.*

SEC. BLUSTER—Where is the reliable Southern gentleman?

PORTER—He is here, sir; but a member of the New York press insists upon seeing you first.

SEC. B.—Insists! did you say?

P.—Yes, sir.

SEC. B.—Ha! There's too much freedom in the word "insists." It smacks of treason, and must be punished. [*Writes an order.*] There! Have him sent forthwith to Lafayette, and now for the reliable gentleman.

[*Porter ushers in the R. S. G.*

R. S. GENTLEMAN—Since my last report I have been placed in possession of further information of a most important character. The Southern Confederacy is rapidly breaking up. Jeff Davis and his cabinet have had a serious quarrel. The women of Richmond have armed themselves to the teeth, and even the children *are in arms.* Boots are selling for a hundred dollars a pair; a single apple can not be had for less than five dollars. Coffee is made of roast sawdust, and very inferior whisky sells at two hundred dollars a gallon. The President's proclamation has set all the negroes rampant, and they are rising and killing their former owners and families. A few days ago Mrs. Davis was heard to say to Jeff, "It's all up with us;" and General Lee, I have heard on reliable authority, is secretly working to make his escape to France.

GEN. M.—Your information, sir, is most valuable, and shall be given to the loyal people of the North without delay. [*Aside*]—As for that office, call on me to-morrow morning, and you shall be duly installed.

SEC. H.—A most intelligent and reliable gentleman that.

ABE L.—Now, gentlemen, you must hurry up, as the old woman will play the deuce if I'm not on hand to meet some friends at dinner. So now to work at that dispatch, and let it be a crusher. Use up the South, or, by thunder! *it may use us up.*

SEC. B.—Gentleman, here is the dispatch ready for the wires.

ABE L.—Ah! Bluster, at the wire-pulling again, old fellow! What do you think of that one, Mallet? Good, wasn't it?

GEN. M.—Capital! excellent! Ha! ha!

ABE L.—That brigadier-generalship is a sure thing. You may bet on it. Now, Bluster, go ahead with your dispatch, and let it be *dispatched* as quick as possible. There's another, Mallet, just got off; another one, old fellow; have you got any more friends you want appointed?

GEN. M.—A few more.

ABE L.—Send in their names; it is as good as done. But read the dispatch.

SEC. B.—(*reads.*)

DISPATCH.

The news from the South is of a most encouraging character, and there are strong indications of a speedy breaking up of the rebellion. A reliable gentleman, just from the heart of Secessia, and who escaped from the almost instant death with which he was threatened, says that very poor whisky is over two hundred dollars a gallon; that, in fact, the South is rapidly losing its *spirits*, and even the women are all in favor of Union—*to a man.* There is a large party in South Carolina who are in favor of bringing back that State, and it was reported that a conspiracy was concocted to give up all the forts in the harbor to Admiral Dupont. The Southern soldiers were generally dissatisfied, and threatened a system of universal desertion. In fact, the rebellion is reduced to a shell, and might be crushed at any time by a vigorous prosecution of the war. It is said that Louis Napoleon advised Jeff Davis to give up, and it is believed that he will have to do so by the end of the next three months, if not sooner.

SEC. H.—That's just the thing. I've no doubt that three months will do for them. Is that all?

SEC. B.—That's all.

ABE L.—Whew! I'm glad of it. Well, Bill, have it sent over the wires, and if our people swallow that dose, anything will stay upon their stomachs.

So now we must away,
And leave the next dispatch for another day.

[*Curtain falls on a grand tableau, representing* SOLOMON GREENBACK *enthusiastically waving a Treasury note, and* MR. LINKEM *reposing in graceful dignity on both chair and table, with his feet and head on a common level, while* GEN. MALLET *and the* RELIABLE SOUTHERN GENTLEMAN *are engaged in a silent conversation.*]

www.ingramcontent.com/pod-product-compliance
Lightning Source LLC
LaVergne TN
LVHW021416110826
845150LV00007B/1954

* 9 7 8 1 4 2 5 5 0 9 6 8 2 *